W9-BBD-173

a girl and her pig

a girl and her pig

APRIL BLOOMFIELD

with JJ GOODE

photographs by david loftus

illustrations by sun young park

ecco

An Imprint of HarperCollins Publishers

A GIRL AND HER PIG. Copyright © 2012 by April Bloomfield. All rights reserved. Printed in China. No part of this book may be used or reproduced in any manner whatsoever without written permission except in the case of brief quotations embodied in critical articles and reviews. For information address HarperCollins Publishers, 10 East 53rd Street, New York, NY 10022.

HarperCollins books may be purchased for educational, business, or sales promotional use. For information please write: Special Markets Department, HarperCollins Publishers, 10 East 53rd Street, New York, NY 10022.

FIRST EDITION

Designed by Suet Chong

Library of Congress Cataloging-in-Publication Data has been applied for.

ISBN 978-0-06-200396-6

13   14   15   16   SCP   10   9   8   7   6   5   4   3

To Rose Gray

contents

acknowledgments

Huge thanks go to the amazing team at Ecco, especially to publisher Daniel Halpern, editor Libby Edelson, interior designer Suet Chong, and art director Allison Saltzman for helping me create a book that I adore.

To my superstar agent, the very handsome Luke Janklow.

To my friend and cowriter, JJ Goode, for his patience and for always pestering me to measure, measure, measure and test, test, test.

To my friend, the immensely talented photographer David Loftus, and to food and prop stylist Georgie Socratous, for lending me a little of their magic.

To the talented Sun Young Park for her incredible illustrations.

To Martin Schoeller for contributing the lovely cover photo.

To Amy Vogler and Jill Santopietro for their careful, thoughtful recipe testing.

To my mentors, past and present, culinary and otherwise: Adam Robinson, Nick Smallwood, Chris Lee, Paul Rankin, Theo Randall, Rowley Leigh, Simon Hopkinson, Rose Gray, Ruthie Rogers, Fergus Henderson, Jamie Oliver, and Mario Batali.

To my wonderful staff, past and present, who kept everything running while I toiled at this book. Special thanks to Peter Cho, Ralphy Johnson, Joshy Schwartz, Katharine Marsh, Dwayne Joseph, Christina Lecki, Preston Miller, Edie Ugot, Charlene Santiago, Scotty Boggs, and Ryan Gannon.

To my friend and partner, Ken Friedman, for taking a chance on a girl from Birmingham, and to Jay-Z, Norman Cook, Paul McGuinness, and Pete Tong for their support.

To my diligent assistant, Emily Stroud, and to my beloved former assistant, Jenn James (and her Bug).

To my great friends Pete Begg, Dolly Sweet, Mike Dowding, and Rachael Smith for their advice, their support, and lots of laughs.

To my wonderful family, my nan and granddad, my mom and dad and sisters. I love you all so much.

To Amy Hou. You're my rock.

Finally, to The Man Upstairs for giving me passion and a second chance.

foreword

April Bloomfield hunches dejectedly over a bowl of meatballs, leaning a cheek on one hand. With the other, she pushes the meatballs around the bowl, eyeing them with great disappointment.

We're on the third floor of The Spotted Pig, her Greenwich Village restaurant, where we've spent more than a year working on this book. She cooks. I watch and ask questions, scribbling down notes or taking video. Today she's made lamb meatballs in a slightly soupy cumin-spiked tomato sauce. At the last minute, she added fresh mint to the pot, dolloped in thick, tangy Greek yogurt, and cracked in a few eggs to poach. When the meatballs were ready, she filled two bowls, passing one to me and keeping the other. I take my first bite and experience a sensation familiar to anyone who has eaten her food: eye-widening, expletive-inducing pleasure. The meatballs are stunning, a dish I thought I knew taken to a new level of deliciousness. Yet she sighs. "Horrible," she says. "These meatballs are horrible."

Spending time in April's kitchen is not typically a melancholy experience. Just the opposite, actually. When she starts cooking, all of her stress—from a broken exhaust hood at The Breslin, the requisite food celebrities stopping in for lunch at The John Dory Oyster Bar, interviews with the media, which she dreads—evaporates, like wine in a hot pan.

As she preps, she looks as though there's nothing she'd rather be doing than peeling shallots or chopping carrots. She practically ogles young onions and spring garlic. She inhales deeply over a pan of sizzling chicken livers, taking in one of her favorite aromas. Browning the lamb meatballs, she's utterly transfixed. "Oh, that lovely color!" she says. "It makes me go all funny in the knickers." There's always a song stuck in her head, and while she works, she'll sing whatever it is in her Brummie brogue: a peek into the oven to check on a roasting lamb's head, the flesh shrinking from its mandible, prompted snippets of the Lady Gaga song that goes,

"Show me your teeth." Whether she's turning an artichoke or filleting anchovies, it's clear she's having fun.

Yet as the meatball episode demonstrates, April battles her own demons in the kitchen. She sets stratospherically high standards, standards so high that even she can't meet them. Her success and torment have a paradoxical relationship: her food is so good because she rarely thinks her food is good enough. When she is happy with the results of her labor, she often denies responsibility, assigning the deliciousness of, say, her roasted carrots to the carrots themselves for being so perfect and sweet. (It's a great tragedy, by the way, that a vegetable savant like April has become best known for burgers and offal. I've never eaten more lovingly prepared vegetables than those from her kitchen.) And she barely eats what she cooks, instead assembling bites and plates for anyone nearby.

April does not impose her will from the kitchen; her lack of egotism leads her to empathize with the people who eat her food. When she composes dishes, she aims to re-create the little moments that bring her joy. Once, just before she whizzed stock and vegetables for a soup, I watched her fish out a slotted-spoonful of carrot chunks, then return them to the pot after blending. "This way," she said, "it's like a little prize when you bite into one later." "Isn't it lovely," she told me, "when you're eating fried rice and you hit some egg? I'll search and search until I find another piece, for another hit of that fatty flavor. Of course, you don't want too much egg— you *want* to have to dig around for it." She cooks like someone who loves to eat.

Watching her reminds me why I love cooking itself, not just the food it produces, and inspires me to spend more time in my own kitchen. The essence of her food is simplicity. The luxe ingredients and ostentatious embellishments that define so much ambitious, "big-city" food are conspicuously absent. Instead, it's unrelenting fastidiousness that defines April's food. A few fussy aspects of preparation— obsessively trimming tomatoes of any pale flesh, making sure each sliver of sautéing garlic turns golden brown, chilling radishes for salad—lead to totally unfussy food. Her marinated peppers and Caesar salad, veal shank and chicken liver toasts are not deconstructed or creatively reimagined dishes. They're exactly what they promise to be, but they taste better than you ever imagined possible.

Like most cookbook readers, I'm not a culinary school grad. Before working with April, I had never made aioli, let alone welcomed a lamb's head into my oven.

Yet now I've served friends almost perfect clones of her cumin-spiked lentil puree, her bright-green pea soup punctuated with little chunks of ham and blobs of crème fraîche, and her veal kidneys tossed in garlic butter. Even my regular everyday cooking has improved since I succumbed to her infectious perfectionism, her attention to the little things. I splurge on salt-packed anchovies, as she does, because they make my food just taste that little bit better that pushes a dish from good to great. I use lemon to add brightness, not necessarily acidity, just as she does. I cut my carrots into oblique chunks so when they're simmered, the edges will be soft but the center will retain its soft crunch and I won't miss out on the joy of chomping on one now and then.

One day, I decided to follow April's recipe for deviled eggs, and I brought them to The Spotted Pig for her to taste. I was terrified, anticipating a meatball moment. Instead, the famously finicky chef pronounced them "quite good." She complimented me as if it were *my* recipe, as if I were responsible for how bracingly cold and vinegary they were. And, in some way, I suppose I was.

JJ Goode

a girl and her pig

introduction

When I was a girl, I wanted to be a policewoman. But then, when I was sixteen, I handed in my application too late. It's funny how a small thing like that can change everything.

I grew up in Birmingham, England, in a neighborhood called Druid's Heath, which sounds like something out of *Lord of the Rings*. It was not that interesting, I'm afraid. Birmingham is an industrial city, the second largest in England. It was a fine place to be a kid, though I'd occasionally feel low about it. Everything there seems to be made of concrete. It's also full of housing estates, massive high-rise flats that are England's version of low-income housing. Quite a few of my family members have lived in housing estates at one point or another, when they were struggling to afford rent. The buildings were all scary and cold and quite grim.

As a teenager, I got hooked on programs like *Cagney & Lacey, CHiPS,* and other cop shows. I know this sounds a bit nerdy, but I wanted to walk the beat, to work as part of a team. I liked rules and structure and repetition, the idea of doing something again and again until I was good at it. I even fantasized about wearing the uniform, although at the time, policewomen weren't allowed to wear trousers: imagine chasing some villain while wearing a skirt.

I'll tell you, I wasn't the brightest bulb in the cupboard. I struggled through my work at senior school (like high school in the United States). I was always serious, and I never missed a day of studies. (I have the attendance awards to prove it.) Still, I preferred to put back pints with my mates at my local pub, staggering home late at night, my eyes squinty like two pissholes in the snow. And, like a prat, I missed my opportunity with the police academy and couldn't apply again for two years. I had to do something in the meantime. My mom sat me down. She suggested I consider becoming a florist. Just then, one of my sisters walked in wearing her cooking school uniform. I thought, I could wear that uniform. Why not have a go at cooking?

Back then, cooking wasn't a way to get your face on the telly. It was a job. To me, making stock, chopping carrots, braising meat, and the like were all just tasks to try to master. My food icons weren't celebrity chefs. Instead, there was my grand-dad, who always cooked a proper fry-up for breakfast: eggs, bacon, sausage, and bread crisped in the fat left in the pan. At school, I ate mountains of boiled potatoes, a knob of butter melting like lava over the top, with a scattering of black pepper like ash. Anything, I thought at the time, was better than my mom's cooking. Now I realize I was a bit hard on her, because she did make an excellent fried egg, brown and crispy at the edges, and the best bacon sandwich, floppy strips crammed between crusty bread and lashed with HP sauce or ketchup.

I loved Sundays. That was when my nan had us over for roast lunch, often pork with all manner of veg, much of it copiously buttered. (The next morning, we'd make "bubble and squeak" with the leftovers, forming little patties and frying them up, then eating them topped with fried egg.) And later, there was tea, not just the drink, but the meal: my dad would set out a spread of cakes, like Battenberg and Mr. Kipling Bakewell Tarts, and crisps and sandwiches of strawberry jam or cucumber or ham.

Since those Sundays in Birmingham, I've met a lot of great cooks and eaten a lot of food that has just blown me away. Yet when I cook today, I draw just as often on the food of my childhood, whether an entire dish or an ingredient or flavor. I think for some people the appeal of the food you once loved fades over time. Not for me: the appeal is still there, as strong as ever, just waiting to be improved upon.

In many ways, I got lucky. I graduated from cooking school during the early days of the gastropub, when entrepreneurs started buying dank old pubs and tearing up the carpets. They installed little kitchens and proper chefs, who turned out rustic ter-rines and lovely slabs of roast beef, cooked to that magical place between rare and medium-rare.

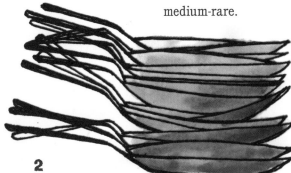

Immediately after graduation, I moved to London, where I got the chance to work for some of the chefs who were leading this movement—among them, Rowley Leigh at Kensington Place, Adam Robinson at The Brackenbury, Simon Hopkinson at Bibendum—and others who were leading movements of their own, like Ruth Rogers and Rose Gray at The River Café. I spent a lot of time listening, and even more watching. I watched how they moved their hands, how they sliced, how they seasoned. I learned that you can make a dish ten times and it will never be the same each time. That just when you think you've mastered something, it'll turn out like a dog's dinner and you realize you haven't really mastered it at all. To this day, I'm always on my toes and always ready to learn something new.

Even after all this time in the kitchen, I still love watching garlic go nutty in hot fat or peeking underneath a piece of caramelizing fennel to see it browning and growing sweeter by the minute. I love spooning pan liquid over roasting meat, piling any vegetable matter on top and gently smooshing it. And as many livers as I've seared in my life, the smell of one meeting a hot pan still makes my knees tremble. The small delights are the most lovely.

My affection for these little things makes me a very particular cook. That's a nice way of admitting that I'm a bit of a control freak. Some of my cooks describe my cooking (affectionately, I hope) as "anal rustic": "rustic" because I prefer pan liquid to complicated sauces, and because I'd rather assemble food by hand than plate it with tweezers, and "anal" because I like everything just so. I must drive my cooks mad when I go on about cutting radishes a certain way to accentuate their slender shape or slicing other vegetables into pieces that taper, so that when they cook, little bits will tumble off into sauce or soup. I sometimes demand that they brown garlic until it's almost too brown or that they not completely cook off alcohol (I like the acidity of slightly raw white wine).

But being a fussy cook doesn't always require more effort. For my pesto, I don't toast the pine nuts—not because of the extra step, but because I find toasting them actually muddies the pesto's flavor. I don't usually peel my beets. Rather, I roast them skins on. I even like to leave on the willowy beet root, which is tender and rustically pretty. For my roasted vegetables, I leave the skins on the onions and garlic, but I peel the carrots. I should really figure out why I peel the carrots.

When you run three restaurant kitchens, trying to make sure the details aren't lost in the race to feed your customers can drive you up the wall. At home, though, there is no such rush. So, for my recipes here, I chose not to gloss over the little things that I think make food taste great and that also make it a pleasure to cook. To that end, the recipes are a little longer than they might otherwise be and, I think, a lot more helpful.

Many of the dishes in this book have shown up in one form or another on my restaurant menus. I'm not much for cooking complicated food, but I do understand that what's straightforward for me and my team of cooks might be a bit knotty for those of you at home just looking for a nice dinner. So, for each dish, I thought, How can I make this more like something an Italian grandma might do? For instance, sometimes I call for using water instead of stock. Or, if at the restaurant we cut vegetables into tiny cubes, I ask you to cut them into chunks. It's easier, the resulting flavor is almost identical, and I think it's quite nice to bite down on a big chunk of carrot or celery here and there.

I've included a few dishes that do take time and effort to make—veal breast stuffed with prosciutto and more veal, cassoulet with duck confit you make yourself, and mussels stuffed with mortadella. They're not difficult to make, but to further encourage you to give them a go, I've included tips for doing some steps in advance.

In general, always read the full recipe before you get started. That way you'll know what to expect and nothing will catch you off guard. You might be tempted to follow a recipe loosely—I know I often am—but on your first go, please try it my way. Then once you've made it one or two times, feel free to tweak it as you'd like. Oh, and always try to use the right pot. I tried to strike a balance between describing the proper pot for a particular dish without being so specific that I scare you off. But do keep in mind that the size and shape of a pot will affect your outcome.

I hope you have as much fun cooking these dishes as I do. And I also hope you'll focus on the little things. Remember, it's easy to make simple food taste great—as long as you don't fuck it up.

my fussy recipes

Before you go headlong into the recipes, I'd like to tell you why they are the way they are. Here I take you through a few of my idiosyncrasies, from the way I think when I cook to the admittedly obsessive measures I take with common pantry staples, and that I urge you to take as well. But, so you don't think I'm a complete nutter, I've given you alternatives whenever I can stomach them.

AT THE MARKET

Please buy great ingredients. I insist on it in my kitchen, and I'm quick to have a fannywobble if the parsnips are spongy or the greens have begun to go limp at the edges. If what you're planning on cooking with doesn't look nice at the market, alter your dinner plans. Talk to your butcher or fishmonger and make it clear that you're after the best he's got. Or order in advance—sometimes that's the best way to be sure that you're buying tasty proteins at their prime. Set your standards high: you might not always meet them, but you will always be better off in the end. Low standards are easy to meet, but the food you'll end up with isn't always good to eat.

Once you've found a great product, get to know it. Taste it raw and as you cook, but first give it a sniff and a good look over. Touch it. The more you do this, the sharper your intuition will become. You'll understand why, for instance, there's no need to peel young carrots and why I urge you to choose fresh sardines with skin that sparkles. That's a good rule of thumb, actually: choose ingredients that sparkle, whether literally or not.

AMOUNTS

I don't like precision. Converting grams to ounces and measuring out tablespoons of chopped parsley does my head in. It feels odd, unnatural, and it's not how I cook.

After all, one carrot or tomato is not the same as another. So you don't want to be inflexible, like a machine. If you open up a pumpkin and it looks a little different than usual, you might have to treat it differently too.

Yet you can't have a cookbook without recipes, and you can't have recipes without measures, so, in the end, I've provided amounts and weights for ingredients I never thought I'd quantify. But where it made sense, I kept the measures called for casual, using handfuls and glugs rather than teaspoons. Use these quantities as guidelines, and use your intuition too.

FINDING THE BALANCE

One summer while I was working at The River Café, I learned a lesson that really stuck. I looked on as Rose Gray, one of the chefs, made ribollita, the Tuscan bread soup. In the winter, we had added a smattering of chopped canned tomatoes to contribute a little acidity. Now it was summer, and we had a glut of ripe, fresh tomatoes. I watched Rose add them with a freer hand. Fresh tomatoes are more delicate, so you have to add more to get the same effect. But just because you have a lot of fresh tomatoes doesn't mean you shouldn't still add them judiciously. What you're after is balance. Finding balance is about understanding a dish's harmonious potential, the place where all the flavors achieve a sort of equilibrium. Each bite should make you want to take another.

Lemon juice is a lovely example of the principle of balance. Of course a dish should never be so lemony that your face scrunches up like a Muppet's as you eat it. But neither should lemon play the same role in every dish. Sometimes lemon's bracing acidity refreshes your palate, as in my Fried Pig's Ear Salad (see recipe, page 86). Other times, lemon just adds brightness, barely perceptible as lemon but vital to encouraging your next eager bite, like in Brussels Sprouts with Pancetta and Juniper Berries (see recipe, page 204).

You must give thought, too, to proportion. A salad with too many walnuts or a sauce with too many capers is like a Sunday with too many free hours— you stop appreciating the pleasure they provide. I think about that when I cook. Put just enough sweet cubes of carrots in a soup, and you won't have to search too hard to find one, but when you do, it'll still give you a little thrill. Always keep in mind why you're adding what you're adding. In Radish Salad (see recipe, page 82), for instance, is the dish about the radish, the cheese, or the combination?

This may all sound a bit tedious. Yet it's how simple food becomes exciting food. And while each recipe in this book aims to guide you toward that elusive place where a dish is in perfect balance, no recipe can account for, say, tomatoes that taste less sweet than you might like or lemons that aren't as tart as usual. Ultimately, the balance is up to you to find.

CUTTING VEGETABLES

In this book, I often ask you to cut vegetables such as carrots and fennel into pieces. What I don't mention, for fear of sounding *too* fussy, is that I typically prefer to cut vegetables into oblique pieces: angled ones with pointy, tapered edges. They're more elegant than clumsy chunks and more rustic than perfect cubes. If you're up for it, here's how to do it: Take, say, a carrot, halve it lengthwise, and set it flat side down. Cut the first piece on a diagonal, then continue slicing into irregular pieces, sliding the carrot back and forth with your other hand between each cut. Keep it up, making sure the pieces are more or less the same thickness.

PLATING

I'm not much for pomp on the plate, for presentation that says, "Look how pretty!" But I do think that if food looks beautiful, people are more excited to eat it. To that end, with most recipes I give suggestions that more or less amount to this rule: Don't serve food in a big, dense lump. Rather, assemble the ingredients so there's a little air flowing between them and any supporting players are scattered here and there among the stars of the dish. I like food to look as if the arrangement were almost accidental, as if it all dropped from above and happened to pile elegantly on the plate.

pluche

INGREDIENTS

HERBS

Because there are few things worse than chomping down on a tough stem. I typically remove any thick, woody stems from herbs.But I don't discard the thin stems close to the leaves, which are sweet and tender. When I use parsley and cilantro in salads, for example, I often pluck sprigs into little lengths, a few inches long, that I once learned are called *pluches.* Herb pluches provide a different experience in each bite than just the leaves would. And a little advice: Always chop fresh herbs right before you use them.

OLIVE OIL

Get yourself a bottle of really good extra virgin olive oil, and use it with abandon. Both a cooking fat and a seasoning, olive oil might be the only ingredient I use as often as Maldon salt. I'll drizzle some over soup at the last minute, add it to bean cooking liquid, or lash it onto slightly charred rustic bread for a snack or side, among a thousand other uses. At home I like to keep a nice mild oil and a peppery one around.

CHILIES

Halfway through writing this book, I started to fret that every recipe had chilies in it. Then I realized that's quite okay. The food isn't spicy—for me, adding chilies, whether dried or fresh, is about adding another layer of flavor, rather than scalding your tongue.

I mainly call for two types of chilies. The first are dried pequin chilies, lovely little things, each one barely bigger than a grain of rice. I love their bright flavor, but if you must, you can substitute red pepper flakes, as long as you replace the bottle often so you don't end up using stale, flavorless ones. For every crumbled pequin chili I call for, you can swap in a pinch of red pepper flakes.

a girl and her pig

The second type is Dutch chili, a slender fresh red chili that's about the size of your pointer finger and a bit spicier than a jalapeño. If you can't find it, use any long, red, moderately spicy chili.

SPICES

There's nothing like buying whole spices and toasting and grinding them yourself. These simple steps amplify their flavor and fragrance. Here's how to do it: Put the spices in a small pan and set it over medium-high heat. (If there's more than one spice in a recipe that requires toasting, I like to do them separately.) Toast, shaking the pan frequently, until the spices smell really sweet and inviting, anywhere from 2 to 4 minutes. Remember that it's less about precise timing than it is about feel—rather than toasting them for 1 minute and 33 seconds, keep a close eye on the spices and take a whiff every now and then. After they're toasted, use your mortar and pestle or spice grinder to reduce them to a powder.

GARLIC

The garlic you get at the store is often a bit old, with little bright green germs growing inside or, if you're really unlucky, peeking out. Whenever I'm chopping garlic, I slice peeled cloves lengthwise and flick this green bit out if I see it. If you don't do this, it won't ruin your dish (though the garlic may turn a blue-green color), and it won't kill you, though it won't make you stronger either.

ANCHOVIES

In some of my dishes, anchovy makes its presence known. In others, it's a bit sneaky, contributing a salty umami quality, the source of which your friends might not be able to finger. Whatever their role, I always use whole salt-packed anchovies of the best quality I can find. Sure, you have to fillet them yourself, but it's quite easy. Plus, they last forever in your fridge. If you must, however, you can substitute the oil-packed kind as long as they're top quality and you gently wipe off the oil from the fillets before you use them.

my fussy recipes

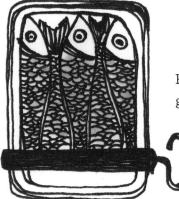

Filleting Salt-Packed Anchovies

Rinse the anchovies one at a time under cold running water, rubbing them gently between your fingers to get the salt off. Put them in a small bowl and add just enough water to cover. After about a minute—if you soak them for too long, they'll lose their umami quality—give them another quick rinse.

To fillet the anchovies, hold an anchovy under cold running water. Pull off the loose muck near the head and at the belly. Rub the outside to remove any remaining salt or hard bits. Keeping the anchovy under the water, gently work a fingertip along the belly to start to separate the fillets. Gently pull the fillets apart—this should be easy, especially once you get the hang of it. Drape the now-boneless fillet over the edge of a bowl to drain. Pinch the backbone and gently pull it away from the second fillet; discard it. Put the second fillet next to the first, and do the same with the rest of the anchovies.

POTATOES

I almost always rinse my potatoes after I chop or peel them, to wash some of the starch away. Doing so helps prevent potatoes from discoloring, keeps mashed potatoes from becoming gluey and sticky, and is just generally a good practice. Here's how I do it: Give the peeled potatoes a rinse under cold running water. Add them to a good-sized pot, run more water over them, and pour it off; repeat if necessary until the water runs clear.

TOMATOES

Nothing gets me grumpy like rubbish tomatoes. You know the kind—bland, crunchy, and paler than my English legs. You don't want to go near a fresh tomato in the winter. And even when you use lovely ripe tomatoes, you should still be fastidious about them, trimming away any pale or hard bits you might spot inside.

I'm equally persnickety about canned tomatoes

a girl and her pig

—or "tinned," as we Brits call them. I urge you to buy the best quality you can. Any brand (I've had good luck with La Valle) whose canned tomatoes you find to be consistently bright in flavor and deep red throughout is a keeper. I also always mean for you to drain off the liquid they come in (unless you're buying those fantastic but expensive jarred tomatoes packed in clear liquid). I find the liquid tastes artificially sweet and salty. Finally, I trim off any horrible bits: yellowish patches, skin, and the tough "eyes." I suggest you do the same.

In several recipes, I call for fresh tomatoes to be blanched and peeled. Here's how to do it: Bring a large pot of water to a boil. Use a knife to make a shallow X through the skin in the bottom of each tomato. Working in batches of tomatoes of similar size, carefully plunge them into the boiling water and blanch for 20 seconds for larger tomatoes, about 10 seconds for small ones. Transfer them to a big bowl of ice-cold water. Drain them and pull the skin off the tomatoes. You can gently scrape them with a knife to loosen any stubborn skin. Cut out the tough core, unless you're working with cherry or grape tomatoes.

BEANS

Buy the freshest dried beans you can find. The idea of "fresh dried beans" might sound like a contradiction, but many of the dried beans you find on supermarket shelves have been dried for so long that they take forever to cook and never achieve the same lovely texture as fresh dried beans. You can identify old beans by looking for bags where lots of beans have begun to crack and split. But your best bet is buying from a reliable source, a brand or shop that has sold you nice beans in the past.

MALDON SALT

When people ask me to name my favorite ingredient, I think about shell beans and ramps, artichokes and parsnips, tomatoes and Parmesan, but in the end I always go with Maldon salt. Made by a 200-year-old English company, the clean-tasting, delicately crunchy flakes of salt are carefully gleaned from the Blackwater River estuary in Essex. I use it to season just about everything, whether at the last minute, so as to preserve a bit of the salt's crunch, or earlier on. Really, the only times I prefer kosher salt are for seasoning meat (a sprinkle of Maldon crystals would tumble right off) or salting pasta water or a brine (who can afford Maldon salt for that!). That said, if you don't have it on hand, another flaky sea salt will do.

BREAD

Filone, a crusty Italian loaf with an airy crumb, is my bread of choice. But if you can't find it locally, you can substitute any bread with similar qualities when you make the following:

Bread Crumbs

When I call for bread crumbs, I mean stale bread (two days or so old) pulsed in a food processor until it's coarse (about the size of lentils) or fine (slightly larger than grains of sand), depending on the recipe. If you don't have stale bread, you can replicate the texture by popping the bread into a low oven for a bit, until it's slightly dried out but hasn't colored.

Toast and Bruschetta

The crunch and heft of toast and simple bruschetta provide perfect contrast to countless dishes, including many in this book. To make toast, I like to grill or griddle slices (about half an inch thick) of crusty rustic bread until they're crunchy on the outside, but not dry and brittle. To make bruschetta, rub one side of each toast liberally with a raw clove of garlic, drizzle with good olive oil (ideally a grassy, peppery oil), and sprinkle with Maldon or another flaky sea salt.

Croutons

I make croutons from stale rustic Italian bread, the crust removed, with a light, hole-riddle crumb, for Caesar Salad (see recipe, page 75) and Roast Chicken with Tomato-and-Bread Salad (see recipe, page 122). The toasting process is the same, but I like croutons of a slightly different shape for these recipes. For the Caesar, I tear enough of the crumb to make two generous handfuls of irregular bite-sized pieces. For the bread salad, I tear the crumb of a large loaf into long strips of different lengths. It's nice for them to be about the same width (about 1 inch), so they toast evenly.

To make the croutons: Spread the bread pieces on a tray in one layer and bake them in a 400°F oven, shaking the pan and tossing the pieces now and then, until they're golden brown and crunchy all the way through, 10 to 15 minutes; they shouldn't give at all when you squeeze them. Keep a close eye on them to be sure they don't get too dark.

EQUIPMENT

MEAT GRINDER

I'm a big fan of grinding my own meat. It gives you control over the cuts of meat you use for burgers and meatballs. It also lets you be sure that the ground meat you cook with hasn't been overworked, which can make the results dense and unappealing. I have the proper grinder at the restaurants, but you can buy a grinder attachment for your stand mixer. Before you grind, I suggest you pop the meat and the grinder attachment into the freezer until the edges of the meat go crunchy. Several recipes in this book ask you to grind meat along with other ingredients, like bread crumbs and herbs. I suggest that you make the effort and do it yourself, but sure, you could ask a nice butcher to do it for you.

MORTAR AND PESTLE

I'd trade all the fancy blenders and mixers in the world for a granite mortar and pestle. I use mine often for pounding toasted spices to a powder, smashing garlic to a paste to make aioli, and much more. You can get by without one—whizzing spices in a grinder, chopping and scraping ingredients to a paste on a cutting board with a chef's knife—but nothing else is quite as satisfying.

breakfast

PANCAKES WITH BACON AND CHILI

Shrove Tuesday is the day before Ash Wednesday. In Britain, we also call it Pancake Day. Traditionally, many families, anticipating the upcoming fast, took Shrove Tuesday as their last opportunity to cook with lovely things like eggs and sugar and butter. Although my family didn't fast, my mom always made these crepe-like pancakes come Shrove Tuesday. They're quite thin and crisp at the edges. You've got to flip them delicately, with a deft flick of your wrist. My mom once tossed one so high that it stuck to the ceiling.

The pancakes take some time at the stove, but the process is satisfying—you'll find yourself getting better at flipping with each one. By the end, you'll have quite a stack. My mom used to serve them sprinkled with sugar and Jif lemon juice from a squeeze bottle shaped like the fruit. I prefer to eat mine drizzled with maple syrup (especially the bourbony kind from Blis Gourmet) and sprinkled with crumbled chili, with some salty, floppy bacon on the side. I love to stack them up and cut them into wedges to serve them, so you are eating twenty-four layers in each bite.

serves 4 (makes 24 pancakes)

FOR THE BATTER

½ pound (1¾ cups) all-purpose flour

Kosher salt

4 large eggs

1¾ cups whole milk

4 tablespoons unsalted butter, melted

FOR THE PANCAKES

About 8 tablespoons (1 stick) unsalted butter, melted,
plus 1 tablespoon or so butter for finishing

Extra virgin olive oil

12 slices bacon

Maple syrup

Dried pequin chilies or red pepper flakes

Make the batter: Sift the flour into a large mixing bowl and stir in 2 pinches of salt. Make a well in the center of the flour and crack the eggs into it, then slowly but steadily whisk in the milk and ¾ cup water (start whisking from the center, and you won't get lumps) until you have a smooth, liquidy batter. Whisk in the 4 tablespoons of melted butter.

Make the pancakes: Heat an 8-inch nonstick pan over high heat for 2 minutes, so it gets nice and hot. Take the pan off the heat and spoon in a little melted butter, a little less than a teaspoon, swirling it around the pan. Then, still off the heat, pour in just enough batter to coat the pan in a thin, almost translucent layer—a generous 2 tablespoons—quickly swirling to disperse the batter evenly (a few bare spots are okay). Return the pan to the heat and cook the pancake, without messing with it, just until the edges begin to brown and lift away from the pan, about 30 seconds. Firmly but carefully shake the pan and, with a deft flick of your wrist, flip the pancake. (You can also use a spatula to lift an edge of the pancake and flip it with your fingers.) Cook it on the second side for 30 seconds, or until both sides are splotched with light golden brown. Transfer it to a plate. Continue cooking the pancakes, stirring the batter and adding a scant teaspoon of the melted butter to the pan between each one, and stacking the pancakes on the plate as you go. They'll keep each other warm until you finish, though it helps to keep the plate in a warm oven.

Pour a few glugs of olive oil into a large pan and set it over high heat. Once the oil begins to smoke, add 4 slices of the bacon. After a minute or so, add the rest (or work in batches to avoid crowding the pan). Cook until the slices are slightly crispy and brown at the edges but still a bit floppy, 3 to 4 minutes. Transfer the bacon to paper towels to drain.

Drizzle the pancake stack with maple syrup, top with a knob of butter, broken up into little pieces, and crumble on as many chilies as you'd like. Serve cut into wedges, with the bacon on the side.

a fried egg

My mom isn't good at cooking much, but she makes the best fried egg sandwich. She gets the egg really crispy and golden around the edges, and now that's how I cook mine. The key is to get your pan and oil nice and hot, so that when the egg hits the hot fat, it sizzles and spits. I sprinkle the setting white and gleaming yolk with Maldon salt, crushed between my fingers. I like my eggs spicy, so they also get some crumbled pequin chili. I can't stand snotty whites—there's nothing worse—so I'll often cover the pan for a few seconds as the egg fries, or baste it with hot fat.

I love a fried egg on toasted crusty bread, perhaps with bacon that's a little crisp but still floppy (I find that when bacon or pancetta is very crispy, you can't taste the pork). And I love a fried egg on bubble and squeak, the yolk spilling over the top with a poke from your fork.

A lot of people like to eat two eggs at a sitting. I like to eat one. One is perfect.

SQUASH AND PANCETTA TOASTS WITH FRIED EGGS

Right before The Pig opened, I was working eighteen hours a day with my sous-chef and a line cook, trying to get everything ready. For a week, we operated on four hours of sleep a night and practically nothing to eat. We were so busy we didn't notice. This is what I cooked for our first real meal, which I guess you'd call breakfast. There's sweetness from the squash, heat from the chili, sweet-and-salty from the pancetta, and creamy relief from the egg. I like to scoop a big hunk of squash, pop it onto the toast, and smoosh it down, leaving some smooth and some with a little texture.   **serves 4**

2 medium garlic cloves, smashed and peeled

2 heaping tablespoons marjoram leaves

4 teaspoons coriander seeds, toasted and ground
(see Spices, page 9)

½ cup plus 3 tablespoons extra virgin olive oil

Maldon or another flaky sea salt

8 or so dried pequin chilies or pinches of red pepper flakes

One 1½-pound butternut squash,
halved lengthwise and seeds scooped out

8 thin slices pancetta

4 large eggs

4 Bruschetta (see Toast and Bruschetta, page 12)

Preheat the oven to 450°F.

Chop the garlic with the marjoram until you have a very fine, well-blended mixture. Combine this mixture with the ground coriander, ½ cup of the olive oil, and 1 tablespoon salt in a large mixing bowl. Crumble in 5 of the chilies and stir well.

Put the squash, one half at a time, into the bowl and use your hands to coat it all over with the oil and seasonings. Put the halves cut sides up in a baking dish and drizzle them with any oil left in the bowl. Pour ½ cup water around the squash, cover the dish tightly with two layers of foil, and pop it into the oven. Roast the squash until you can slide a knife into the thickest part of the flesh without resistance, about 45 minutes. Remove the foil, flip the squash halves so the cut sides face down, and roast for about 10 minutes more, until the cut sides are just a bit brown. Set the dish aside in a warm place.

Pour the remaining 3 tablespoons olive oil into a medium nonstick pan and set it over high heat. Once the oil begins to smoke, add 4 slices of the pancetta. Once they shrink up, add the rest. Cook the pancetta, stirring it a bit, until it's brown at the edges but still floppy, 3 to 4 minutes. Transfer to paper towels to drain, and reserve the fat in a bowl.

Scoop out the squash with a spoon and spread a good bit of it on each bruschetta.

Pour some of the pancetta fat (a generous tablespoon per egg) back into the pan (fry the eggs in two batches if you must) and set it over medium-high heat. When the fat is barely smoking, crack the eggs into the pan. You should hear spitting and sizzling when you add them. That means the whites will get crispy on the edges. When the whites begin to set, sprinkle the eggs with a little salt and as much crushed chili as you'd like. Cook the eggs as you prefer—I like mine over easy for this recipe, with runny yolks.

Top each bruschetta with an egg and then 2 slices of the pancetta. Serve straightaway.

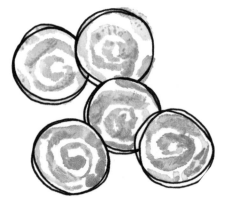

BAKED EGGS WITH ANCHOVIES AND CREAM

On those rare relaxed mornings when I have the time to flip through the paper, I make myself these baked eggs. Cream and anchovies make a lovely couple—the result isn't fishy. Rather, the anchovy fades into the background, sneaking its salty umami quality into every bite. I like to dip my spoon in and spread the eggs on olive oil–lashed charred slices of crusty bread.   **serves 4**

1 large garlic clove, crushed and peeled

1 teaspoon rosemary leaves

About 2 tablespoons unsalted butter

3 whole salt-packed anchovies, rinsed, soaked, and filleted
(see Filleting Salt-Packed Anchovies, page 10)

6 tablespoons heavy cream

¼ teaspoon finely grated lemon zest

4 large eggs

A few dried pequin chilies or pinches of red pepper flakes

Maldon or another flaky sea salt

4 teaspoons crème fraîche

Preheat the oven to 400°F.

Finely chop the garlic with the rosemary until the mixture looks a bit like blue cheese.

Put 1 tablespoon of the butter in a medium pan set over medium-high heat and bring it to a froth. Add the garlic and rosemary mixture and give the pan a little shake. When the garlic starts to go brown and nutty, about a minute, add the anchovy fillets, give the pan another little shake, and turn off the heat. Stir the anchovies until they break up. Have a smell—to me, anchovies smell crispy as they cook. Pour in the cream, add the lemon zest, and stir some more. Turn the heat back to medium-high, bring to a boil, then remove from the heat.

Rub four 8-ounce ramekins with the remaining butter. Put the ramekins in a medium baking dish, split the cream mixture evenly among them, and crack an egg into each one. Roughly crumble on the chilies and sprinkle a pinch of salt over each yolk. Add a dollop of crème fraîche to each ramekin. Pour just enough water into the baking dish so the water level reaches a little past the level of the cream in the ramekins.

Carefully transfer the baking dish to the middle rack in the oven and cook just until the whites have set completely and the yolks are still creamy, about 20 minutes. Remove the baking dish from the oven and let the ramekins sit in the water for 2 minutes. Use sturdy tongs to carefully remove them from the water. Serve straightaway.

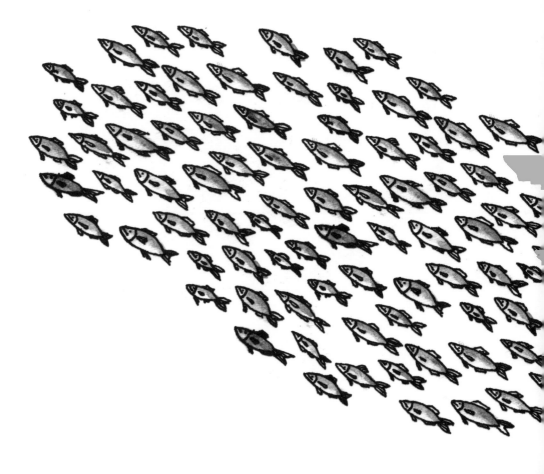

PORRIDGE

My granddad used to make the best porridge (oatmeal to you in the States). When-ever he did, I'd think about Goldilocks: Granddad's porridge was never too runny or too thick—it was always just right. He'd simmer rolled oats in milk, and it always smelled so sweet and inviting. Even today, the thought of it makes me go all warm inside. Next, he'd spoon the porridge into a bowl and let it sit until it formed a little skin and began to pull away from the sides. Then my favorite part: He'd pour milk into the space around the edges, the cool milk hitting the hot porridge and making it set like custard. Finally, he'd sprinkle sugar over the middle. The hot porridge, the crunchy sugar, the moat of milk—it was so comforting. Just the thing for cold morn-ings when there was frost on the ground, and you knew that pretty soon you'd have to leave the house all wrapped up in your scarf, bobble hat, and mitts and pop off to school. These days, I'll sometimes add a bit of crumbled dried chili to my porridge. It goes especially nicely with maple syrup. **serves 4**

1½ cups whole milk, plus a few generous splashes
1½ teaspoons Maldon or another flaky sea salt
½ cup steel-cut oats
½ cup rolled oats (not "quick-cooking" or "instant")
About 2 tablespoons sugar (maple, brown, or white) or maple syrup

Combine the 1½ cups milk, 1½ cups water, and the salt in a medium pot (a 2-quart pot should do it) and set over high heat. As soon as the liquid comes to a gentle sim-mer, add both kinds of oats and lower the heat to medium. Cook the oats at a steady simmer, stirring frequently and tweaking the heat as necessary to maintain the simmer. After about 20 minutes at the simmer, the rolled oats will have turned a bit mushy, while the steel-cut oats will be just tender and pop when you bite them. Turn off the heat.

Have a taste. It's good and salty, isn't it? Now you want to add sugar or syrup to your taste. I like my porridge to taste a little salty at first, then fade into sweet. Spoon the porridge into warm bowls and let it sit for a minute. Then carefully pour a little cold milk around the edges of each bowl, so it pools all the way round. Sprinkle a five-fingered pinch of sugar or drizzle the syrup in the center of each and let it melt, then serve right away.

Note:
This recipe feeds four, but it's great reheated—make the whole batch even if you're just feeding one or two. Reheat leftovers over low heat along with a splash of water or milk.

rose and ruthie

When I was hired at The River Café, Rose Gray and Ruth Rogers were my bosses. By the time I left, they were my mentors and my friends. Rose was seventy-one when she passed away. Just ten months before that, she'd still been working four days a week in the kitchen.

Rose didn't give compliments often, and I actually grew to love that about her. I think that she was just honest. If you were doing a good job, she'd say it. If not, she'd keep mum. I was always doing something embarrassing in front of her. One day, she and I planted zucchini in the restaurant's garden. I'm a Taurus. I'm supposed to have a green thumb. But a few days later, Rose looked at the zucchini she had planted. The plant stood there looking vigorous. She took a look at my sad, droopy, little plant and said, in her thick London accent, "Darling, I think you've killed it."

My first month at The Spotted Pig, Rose came on a visit from England. The night she stopped by, I was on the line with just two other cooks. The Pig's burger had gotten a bit of press, and we had twenty of them grilling at once. I was a mess—sweating, my hair going every which way, like weeds in a garden. That was when Rose chose to pop her head into the kitchen. *Fuck,* I thought, *Rose Gray is here and all I'm doing is cooking burgers!* Her only comment on The Pig was that she didn't care for the raw onion I'd put in a salad.

When you're a young cook with a fragile ego, someone like Rose isn't an easy person to work for, but she was certainly an inspiring one. Rose almost always took a notebook with her when she went out for dinner, especially in Italy. She'd draw little pictures of dishes she liked and scribble down notes on how she thought they were made. The amazing bit is that when she and Ruthie re-created them in the restaurant's kitchen, their versions were even better. They were both so passionate about food. Everything had to be just so, from the way food was plated to the balsamic vinegar they used. It was infectious. I began to believe what they believed. It consumed me, partly because it felt so great to be consumed by. It's why I'm so hard on my cooks today.

The duo's dynamic spirit made me feel lucky to be around them, even during tedious tasks. And I'll never forget the day when there was a plumbing problem (and therefore, a bit of a smell) at the restaurant. I don't know what most people would have done—light candles? spray air freshener?—but straight off, Rose had us put a massive wheel of ripe Gorgonzola out on the bar.

Perhaps my favorite times at The River Café were when Rose and I would meet in the morning to discuss the day's menu. I'd come in, invigorated from my stroll to the restaurant along the Thames and through the restaurant's little garden. It was quiet inside, and I'd have a rare moment to take in where I was. I would make breakfast: toast with olive oil and salted anchovies for Rose. For me, toast rubbed with raw garlic and slathered with leftover vinegary Salsa Verde (see recipe, page 289). Perhaps a little grated Parmesan and a drizzle of Tuscan olive oil. Each bite reminded me how far I'd come from carving roasts at the Holiday Inn.

POTATO BREAD

This is just about the easiest bread to make. The dough doesn't require a mother starter or endless kneading, but despite the lack of effort, the result is a moist, lovely crumb with lots of character and a thin, crispy crust. The bread toasts beautifully and goes just as well with pâtés as it does with Fennel-Lemon Marmalade (see recipe, page 262). It also makes fantastic sandwiches, stuffed with turkey or ham, of course, or perhaps leftover slices of Stuffed Veal Breast (see recipe, page 145).

makes 1 large round loaf

1 pound russet (baking) potatoes, scrubbed and cut into 1-inch pieces
2 teaspoons kosher salt
1 tightly packed tablespoon crumbled fresh yeast or
2¼ teaspoons active dry yeast
2¼ cups all-purpose flour, plus extra for dusting
2 tablespoons extra virgin olive oil, plus a drizzle for the bowl
1 tablespoon Maldon or another flaky sea salt

Special Equipment
A pizza stone; stand mixer with a paddle attachment and a dough hook

Pop the potatoes into a medium pot, pour in just enough water to cover them, and add the kosher salt. Set the pot over high heat and bring the water to a boil, then lower the heat and gently simmer just until the potatoes can be easily pierced with a fork, 10 to 20 minutes. Drain the potatoes in a colander, reserving ¼ cup of the cooking liquid, and let them cool in the colander until tepid.

Put the potatoes in the bowl of a stand mixer fitted with the paddle attachment. Mix on medium speed until the potatoes are crushed but still chunky. Replace the paddle attachment with the dough hook.

Use an instant-read thermometer to measure the temperature of the reserved cooking liquid. Reheat if necessary so it's between 105° and 115°F. Stir the yeast into the liquid until it dissolves, then wait for it to bubble, so you can be sure the yeast is active. This could take up to 5 minutes.

Add the yeast mixture, flour, olive oil, and sea salt to the potatoes and mix on low speed for about 2 minutes, until the mixture has combined. (The dough should be quite sticky to the touch. If it isn't, gradually mix in a little water.) Increase the speed to medium and mix, occasionally stopping the machine to scrape down the sides of the bowl, until you have an elastic dough, about 10 minutes more. It's okay to have a few odd lumps of potato.

Lightly flour your work surface and hands. Transfer the dough to the work surface and knead for 3 minutes. Tuck the edges of the dough underneath it to form a ball. Lightly oil a bowl with olive oil and add the dough to the bowl. Cover the bowl with plastic wrap and let the dough rise at room temperature until it doubles in size, 30 to 50 minutes, depending on the temperature of your kitchen. It helps to put the dough in a warm place, like on the counter near a preheated oven.

Lightly flour your work surface and hands again. Put the dough on the work surface and knead until it looks smooth, about 1 minute, then tuck the edges underneath again to form a ball. Turn the ball over and gently pinch the seam partially closed.

Add a generous amount of flour to your work surface and lay the dough on it seam side down. Cover the dough with a damp (not wet) kitchen towel and let it rise (again, in a warm place) until it's nearly doubled in volume, 25 to 40 minutes.

Meanwhile, put the pizza stone on the center rack of the oven and preheat the oven to 375°F.

Handling the dough gently, place it seam side up on the hot pizza stone and bake, rotating the bread after 20 minutes, until the crust is a deep golden-brown color, about 40 minutes. Another way to tell if it's ready is to gently tap the base of the loaf with your knuckles—if it sounds hollow, it's done. Transfer to a rack to cool. You can eat the bread while it's still slightly warm, but I prefer it after it has cooled completely.

A NOTE ON YEAST

When I make bread, I use crumbly little blocks of fresh yeast, also known as cake yeast. But this type of yeast is not always available to home cooks. If you've asked around at your local bakery and come up empty, use active dry yeast, which is easy to find and far less perishable. Either way, store any extra yeast in the freezer, where it'll keep for a long time.

nibbles

DEVILED EGGS

I like my deviled eggs cold, cold, cold. They're so refreshing that way. The key to the recipe is chilling the whites as well as the yolk mixture and making your own mayonnaise, which is much easier than you might think.   **makes 12 deviled eggs**

6 large eggs, at room temperature
3 tablespoons Mayonnaise (see recipe, page 297), slightly chilled
1 tablespoon champagne vinegar
1 tablespoon crème fraîche
1 teaspoon Dijon mustard
Maldon or another flaky sea salt
2 tablespoons finely chopped chives
1 tablespoon finely chopped chervil
Cayenne or paprika
Extra virgin olive oil (optional) for drizzling

Fill a medium pot at least halfway with water and bring to a boil over high heat. Use a slotted spoon to gently put the eggs in the water, and cook them for 10 minutes (set a timer). Drain the eggs and put them in a big bowl of ice water until they're fully cool.

Lightly tap each egg against the counter to crack the shell all over, then peel them and pat them dry. Halve them lengthwise with a sharp knife.

Press the yolks through a sieve into a small food processor. Add the mayonnaise, vinegar, crème fraîche, and mustard and process until smooth, scraping down the sides as necessary. Have a taste and season with salt.

For really pretty eggs, feed the mix into a pastry bag (alternatively, you can jerry-rig one with a large resealable plastic bag; snip off a corner before piping). Pop it into the fridge for 30 minutes. Put the egg whites on a plate, cover with plastic wrap, and put them in the fridge as well.

Pat the whites dry with a kitchen towel and pipe an equal amount of the yolk mixture into each white. Top each one off with a sprinkle of the chives and chervil and a dusting of cayenne or paprika. If you like, add a sprinkle of sea salt and a drizzle of olive oil and serve.

CHOPPED CHICKEN LIVER ON TOAST

A staple at The Spotted Pig, this creamy, still slightly chunky mash of lovely, iron-y livers on toast makes a fine snack, but it's substantial enough to hold you over while you wait for a friend or a table. Just the thing, too, with a glass of wine. The liver mixture is a touch sweet from the port and the browned garlic and shallots, with a whisper of acidity from the Madeira. Best of all, it takes just a moment to make. Be sure you get a nice color on the livers when you cook them. (I like them slightly pink on the inside for this dish; anyone who doesn't can cook them a bit longer.) Be sure to take in the aroma as they cook—toasty browning liver is one of my favorite smells.   **makes 4 toasts**

About ¼ cup extra virgin olive oil, plus more for drizzling
Heaping ¼ cup finely chopped shallots
1 large garlic clove, thinly sliced
2 tablespoons dry Madeira
2 tablespoons ruby port
½ pound chicken livers, trimmed and separated into lobes
Maldon or another flaky sea salt
Freshly ground black pepper
A small handful of small, delicate flat-leaf parsley sprigs
4 thick slices crusty bread, or 2 large slices, cut in half

Pour 2 tablespoons of the olive oil into a large sauté pan and set it over high heat. When it's hot, turn the heat down to medium and add the shallots and garlic. Cook until they're golden brown, about a minute. Add the Madeira and port to the pan and give it a good shake, then scrape the mixture into a small bowl and set aside.

Rinse the pan and wipe it out well with a paper towel, then set it over high heat and add 1 tablespoon of the olive oil. When the oil just begins to smoke, pat the livers dry and add them to the pan. Cook until the undersides are golden brown, 1½ minutes or so. Carefully turn them over and sprinkle on about 1 teaspoon salt, then give the pan a little shake. Cook the livers just until they feel bouncy, like little balloons, about 30 seconds more. You want them slightly pink inside, not rare.

Turn off the heat and add the shallot mixture, liquid and all, to the pan.

Shake the pan, stirring and scraping it with a spoon to loosen the crispy brown bits on the bottom, then scrape the contents of the pan into a bowl. Let it all cool for a few minutes.

Drizzle about 1 tablespoon olive oil over the liver mixture and sprinkle in about a teaspoon of salt and a couple twists of black pepper. Use a large spoon to chop, stir, and mash the livers until some of the mash is creamy and some is still a little chunky. Coarsely chop the parsley, add it to the liver mixture, and give it all a good stir. Let it cool to room temperature.

Toast or grill the bread until crispy but still a bit soft in the middle. Drizzle the toasts with a little olive oil, spread on a generous amount of the liver mixture, and serve straightaway.

OLIVES WITH TOMATOES AND PRESERVED LEMON

I love thinking up new ways to serve Castelvetrano olives, rather than just plunking the bright-green, fleshy orbs on a plate. Like turning them into this colorful snack, where you get to experience their distinctive flavor in a refreshing tomato sauce with the zing of preserved lemon. **serves 4**

2 tablespoons extra virgin olive oil

2 garlic cloves, very thinly sliced

½ small preserved lemon, pith and flesh discarded, rind thinly sliced

Small pinch of saffron threads

One 15-ounce can peeled whole tomatoes, drained, trimmed, and pureed

1 large Dutch or other spicy long red chili

¼ teaspoon cumin seeds, toasted and ground (see Spices, page 9)

½ pound drained Castelvetrano olives

Small pinch of Maldon or another flaky sea salt

Heat the oil in a small pot that has a lid over medium-high heat until it just begins to smoke. Add the garlic and cook, stirring often, until light golden brown and toasty, about 1 minute. Add the preserved lemon rind and saffron and stir well, then add the tomatoes, turn the heat down to low, and cover the pot. Cook for 10 minutes or so, to let the flavors meld.

Meanwhile, turn a gas burner to medium-high and use tongs to roast the chili directly over the burner, turning often, until it's blistered all over with just a few black spots, about 2 minutes. Scrape off the skin with a knife, then cut off the stem, scrape out and discard the seeds, and roughly chop the chili.

Add the chili, cumin, olives, and salt to the pot (leave it uncovered), adjust the heat to maintain a gentle simmer, and cook, stirring often, until the tomato starts clinging to the olives, about 10 minutes. Scrape it all into a bowl and let cool to room temperature.

Serve, or keep in the fridge for up to 4 days. Let it come to room temperature, and stir well before serving.

ROASTED PEANUTS WITH ROSEMARY AND GARLIC

At The Breslin, we serve snacks like scrumpets, which are breaded and deep-fried shreds of fatty lamb, and boiled peanuts fried in pork fat. But at The John Dory, I wanted the bar snacks to be a bit lighter, more appropriate as preludes to platters of oysters and bowls of razor clam ceviche. So I came up with these salty, roasty peanuts tumbled with slightly crispy rosemary and sweet, soft cloves of garlic, rustic in their papery skins. It's a nice thing to set out at a party or to nibble on while watching a movie. **makes about 3 cups**

¼ cup extra virgin olive oil
12 skin-on garlic cloves
½ cup lightly packed rosemary leaves
3 cups salted skin-on roasted peanuts, preferably small Spanish peanuts
1 tablespoon Maldon or another flaky sea salt, or more to taste
5 or so dried pequin chilies or pinches of red pepper flakes

Heat the olive oil in a wide pan with high sides over medium-high heat until it just begins to smoke. Add the garlic cloves, adjust the heat if necessary to cook them at a steadily sizzle, and cook, tipping the pan occasionally so the oil pools and almost covers the cloves, until the garlic has some golden brown spots and the skins begin to split and blister, about 5 minutes.

Push the garlic to one side of the pan, put the rosemary in the oil next to the garlic, and add the peanuts to the space remaining in the pan. Turn the heat down to medium and let the rosemary sizzle in the oil for a minute, stirring it a little, then stir it together with the peanuts and garlic. Let them all quietly and steadily sizzle together—you're infusing the flavors of the garlic and rosemary into the peanuts, cooking the garlic more so it'll be soft and creamy, and reinvigorating the roasted peanuts—stirring and tossing the peanuts often, so they all get to spend some time against the bottom of the pan, about 5 minutes. About a minute before that, sprinkle on the salt, crumble in the chilies, and stir well.

Take the pan off the heat and let the peanuts carry on cooking gently in the hot pan, stirring now and then, until they've cooled a bit. Have a taste, and stir in a little more salt or crumbled chilies if you fancy it. Serve warm or at room temperature.

nibbles **41**

TOASTS WITH RAMP BUTTER
AND FRIED QUAIL EGGS

Ramps are lovely, slender wild leeks. They have a white bulb that turns to purple as it meets the stem, which then develops into a delicate green leaf. I get really excited when ramps finally arrive at the market because it means spring is coming—open your windows, clean out your cupboards!—and my winter funk is over. Early in the season, when ramps are especially sweet and tender (later on they're bigger and starchy), I make a simple butter that combines the nutty sweetness of the bulbs and the fresh leeky taste of the tops. Each bite is a little different: in some you taste spikes of lemon; in others, sweetness; and in still others, saltiness. Ramp butter is the sort of thing that's good on just about everything—dolloped on mashed potatoes, spread on lamb chops, or tossed with pasta. (Ramps have this "more-ish" smell, as we say in England—that is, they smell so good you want more.) But I especially love it slathered on toasted bread and topped with a quail egg, a more exciting version of the boiled egg and soldiers I ate for breakfast as a kid in Birmingham. **makes 8**

A scant ¼ pound ramps, roots trimmed

11 tablespoons unsalted butter, at room temperature

Maldon or another flaky sea salt

3 whole salt-packed anchovies, rinsed, soaked, and filleted (see Filleting Salt-Packed Anchovies, page 10), then finely chopped

1 tablespoon finely grated lemon zest (from about 2 large lemons)

1½ teaspoons freshly squeezed lemon juice, or more to taste

A few glugs of extra virgin olive oil

Dried pequin chilies or red pepper flakes

Freshly ground black pepper

Eight ½-inch-thick diagonal slices from a baguette, toasted and cooled

8 quail eggs

Pile the ramps on your cutting board so the bulb ends line up. Start by thinly slicing the bulbs, working your way toward the green leaves. After you've sliced the purple stems and reached the greens, make your slices even thinner. Gather the sliced bulbs and stems into a little pile. Set the greens aside for the moment.

Put 1 tablespoon of the butter in a sauté pan and set it over medium-high heat. Once it melts and froths, add the sliced ramp bulbs and stems (along with a five-fingered pinch of greens) and a sprinkle of salt. Cook, stirring often, until the ramps have a hint of brown, 2 minutes or so.

Scrape the ramps into a bowl and add the remaining 10 tablespoons butter, the anchovies, lemon zest, lemon juice, a glug of olive oil, a few crumbled chilies, and, if you fancy, a few twists of black pepper. Mash, toss, and stir the mixture with a fork or wooden spoon just until everything's nicely mixed. Give the reserved ramp greens a brief chop, then stir them in. Have a taste. You should taste the gentle onion flavor of the ramps, a good bit of umami-saltiness from the anchovies, and brightness, not tartness, from the lemon. To me, this butter tastes like spring. You might want to add another ¼ teaspoon salt or another brief squeeze of lemon. (You can refrigerate the butter for a day or two in a bowl, or roll it into a log, if you're feeling fancy.)

Slather the toasts with the ramp butter (you'll have extra butter; reserve it for another day).

Pour a glug or two of oil into a nonstick pan just large enough to hold the eggs comfortably (you can also fry them in 2 batches) and set it over medium-high heat. When the oil is barely smoking, crack the eggs into the pan. (It helps to insert the tip of a knife into the shell, though not so far in that you break the yolk.) You should hear spitting and sizzling when you add them. Cook them until the whites are set and golden brown at the edges but the yolks are still runny, about a minute.

Top each toast with a quail egg and add a little sprinkle of salt. Serve straightaway.

CLEANING RAMPS

Ramps are usually a bit dirty when you buy them, so you need to wash them well—but please handle them with care. They're special little things and delicate too. It'd be a shame to bruise them. Fill a big bowl with cold water and add the ramps. Swish them around gently and rub them carefully with your fingers to dislodge any dirt on the leaves and to remove any mushy layer on the bulbs. Change the water two or three times until you're satisfied, then gently shake the ramps and lay them on a kitchen towel to dry.

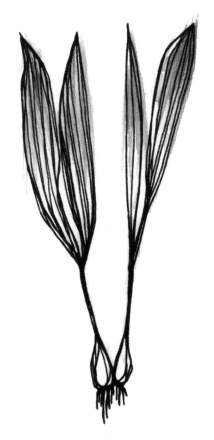

DEVILS ON HORSEBACK

We serve these bacon-wrapped prunes at The Spotted Pig, and they go down a treat—salty, sweet, meaty, and the ultimate snack for soaking up whatever alcohol you might be drinking. I marinate the prunes first in a little tea, which plumps them and balances their sweetness with a touch of bitterness. (I'd happily spoon the voluptuous fruit and its liquid onto yogurt.) The aroma of the roasting fruit and bacon will fill your house, so it's particularly nice to cook these just before friends arrive. You'll use only a small portion of the pears prepared here, but there are so many other ways to eat them. My two favorites are tossing the sweet-tart slices with toasted walnuts in a salad of hearty lettuces or serving them alongside a nice hunk of blue cheese.   **makes 10**

FOR THE PEARS
2 cups dry white wine, such as Sauvignon Blanc

1 cup white wine vinegar

1 cup superfine sugar

1 tablespoon sliced skin-on fresh ginger

10 black peppercorns

4 whole allspice berries

About 4 dried pequin chilies or pinches of red pepper flakes

1 large cinnamon stick

3 large perfectly ripe Bartlett pears

FOR THE PRUNES
1 English Breakfast tea bag, preferably PG Tips brand

3 tablespoons Armagnac or Cognac

10 large pitted prunes

10 thin slices bacon

Maldon or another flaky sea salt

2 or 3 dried pequin chilies or pinches of red pepper flakes

For the pears: Combine the first eight ingredients in a pot just big enough for the pears to be submerged in the liquid in a snug fit. One at a time, peel the pears and halve them lengthwise. Use a small spoon to scoop out the tough core from each pear half, then trim off the hard bit at the base of each one. As you finish prepping each one, add it to the liquid so it doesn't brown.

Bring the liquid to a boil over medium-high heat, then turn down the heat so it simmers gently (don't rush it, or the pears will disintegrate). Cook just until the pears are tender but not very soft or mushy, 15 to 20 minutes, depending on the firmness of the pears.

Turn off the heat and let the pears cool in the liquid. They'll continue to cook a bit as they cool. Once cool, they'll still have a touch of snap to them, a soft crunch. They'll keep happily in their liquid in an airtight container in the fridge for up to 2 weeks.

For the prunes: Bring 1 cup of water to a boil in a small pan. Add the tea bag and let steep for 5 minutes, off the heat. Discard the tea bag and let the tea cool completely.

Combine the tea, Armagnac, and prunes in a small bowl. The prunes should be completely submerged in the liquid; if they're not, use a different container. Cover the bowl with plastic wrap and pop it into the fridge. Let the prunes soak just until they're plump and soft, overnight or longer if necessary.

When the prunes are ready, remove them from the liquid. Reserve 2 tablespoons of the liquid.

Cut half of one of the spiced pears into 10 oblique pieces that will fit inside the prunes but are not so small that the prune envelops it completely. You want an inch or so of the pear to peek out at one end of the prune. Stuff each prune with a pear piece. You might have to pop your little finger into the prune first.

Lay a slice of bacon on a cutting board, put a prune at one end, and roll up so the prune is wrapped in the bacon. If you feel there's too much bacon, cut a little off—you want a nice balance between bacon and prune. Repeat with the remaining prunes and bacon. Covered with plastic wrap, they keep overnight.

Position a rack in the middle of the oven and preheat the broiler (if you don't have a broiler, heat the oven to 500°F).

Arrange the prunes seam side down in a shallow baking pan, leaving some room between them. Add 3 tablespoons of the pear liquid to the pan, along with the reserved prune liquor, then add a generous pinch of salt and crumble in the chilies. Baste, then cook the prunes under the broiler, basting them with the liquid every few minutes or so, until the bacon is golden and slightly crispy, about 15 minutes. Transfer the prunes to a plate or tray and drizzle with some of the liquid. If your bacon is on the sweet side, sprinkle on salt to taste. Let cool slightly before you dig in.

MARINATED SARDINES

The sardine might be my favorite fish, and as much as I love them grilled whole, this is also a fantastic way to eat them. Marinating the fillets in a simple mixture of little more than lemon juice and olive oil firms them up and lends them a brightness that doesn't interfere with their oceanic quality. The result is refreshing and cleanly flavored. The sardines are a treat laid over a salad of tomatoes or on top of some sliced cucumber tossed with crème fraîche and dill, though I often just eat them on olive oil–lashed toast, perhaps with a little arugula and crumbled chili.   **serves 4**

¼ cup plus 1 tablespoon freshly squeezed lemon juice
A generous pinch of finely grated lemon zest
3 dried pequin chilies, crumbled, or pinches of red pepper flakes
1 teaspoon kosher salt
8 large fresh sardines (about 1 pound), scaled, gutted, and filleted
(see Buying and Filleting Sardines, page 49)
3 tablespoons extra virgin olive oil
A small handful of small, delicate flat-leaf parsley sprigs

Combine the lemon juice, zest, chilies, and salt in a medium dish that's at least an inch deep and just large enough to fit the sardines in one layer. Gently shake the dish and swirl the liquid to dissolve the salt. Gently lay the sardine fillets skin side up in the mixture. You don't want to stir them, because agitating them too much will release their oil and you'll get a slightly fishier flavor.

Drizzle the olive oil over the top. Give the dish a gentle shake to make sure the sardines have settled in the liquid and look comfortable. They won't quite be submerged.

Cover the dish with plastic wrap and pop it into the fridge overnight. The lemon will cook the sardines, firming them up a bit and infusing them with its flavor. (You can leave them to marinate for up to 2 days. They'll be quite firm but still tasty.) Before serving, take them out of the fridge for a few minutes. I like to eat them when they still have a slight chill to them. Roughly chop the parsley and sprinkle it on the sardines. However you serve them, make sure to top them with a drizzle of the pan liquor.

BUYING AND FILLETING SARDINES

Choose fresh sardines that have firm flesh, clear eyes, and shiny skin. Their scales should be tight against their bodies, not flaking off. Ask your fishmonger to fillet them or, even better, do it yourself. Rinse the sardines under running water, rubbing them gently to remove any stray scales, then pat them dry. Get a small sharp knife, preferably a flexible one like a fillet knife. Put the sardines on a cutting board. Hold your knife perpendicular to a fish and insert it into the flesh just behind the head. Grip the head with your other hand and use a gentle sawing motion to cut along the backbone toward the tail to remove the first fillet. Flip the fish over and do the same to the other side. Repeat with the rest of the sardines. Lay each one skin side down on the cutting board and trim off any fins, hard bits, or dark bits from the edges. Leave the thin bones be. They'll dissolve as the fish marinate.

CARTA DA MUSICA WITH BOTTARGA AND BUTTER

I had the great pleasure of eating this for the first time at Marcella Hazan's house. Before serving a stunningly simple veal shank (see Dinner with Marcella, page 148), she set out crispy disks of paper-thin flatbread that she'd brushed with butter and showered with shavings of slightly caramel-y bottarga, the salted dried roe of the gray mullet. We ate them pressed against each other, like slim sandwiches.

She told us that the bread, a Sardinian treat, is called *carta da musica*, which translates as "sheet of music," because of its fragile thinness (it is known as *pane carasau* in the Sardinian dialect). Carta da musica is ingenious, really: a simple dough that puffs up like a balloon in the oven, which you then separate into two thin layers that are baked again until they go crispy. Your task is to make sure you roll the dough to an even thickness and lay it nice and flat on a hot pizza stone. You'll quickly get the hang of it. **makes 12 little sandwiches**

FOR THE DOUGH

½ cup all-purpose flour, plus extra for dusting

½ cup very fine semolina flour

¼ teaspoon kosher salt

FOR THE SANDWICHES

3 tablespoons unsalted butter, at room temperature

3 ounces Sardinian gray mullet bottarga, very thinly sliced at the last minute on a mandoline

Maldon or another flaky sea salt

1 or 2 dried pequin chilies, crumbled, or pinches of red pepper flakes (optional)

Extra virgin olive oil for drizzling

Special Equipment
Pizza stone; mandoline

Make the dough: Mix the flours and salt in a mixing bowl and make a well in the center. Slowly pour in ¼ cup room-temperature water, stirring it in with a fork. Use the fork to mix gradually, adding more water if necessary, until all the flour is incorporated and you have a smooth, barely moist, firm but pliable dough.

Lightly dust a work surface with flour, put the dough on the work surface, and knead it until it's as smooth as a baby's bum, about 7 minutes.

Roll the dough into a log that's about 6 inches long and 2 inches thick. Wrap it in plastic wrap and let rest for at least 2 hours or overnight in the fridge.

Preheat the oven to 450°F. Put an oven rack in the lower third of the oven and remove any other racks. Put a pizza stone on the rack and let it get good and hot, at least 20 minutes. If it's not really hot, your dough won't puff up like a balloon, which is essential.

Dust your work surface with plenty of flour. Cut the log into six 1-inch-thick pieces and cover them with a barely damp kitchen towel. Working with one at a time, on the floured surface, roll each disk into a thin, even circle about 6 inches in diameter. Even thickness is important; otherwise, the circles won't puff up.

Make the carta da musica: One or two at a time, carefully lay the disks on the hot pizza stone so they lie completely flat, with no folds, bumps, or creases, or (guess what?) they won't puff up. Bake until they begin to bubble, then start to puff, about 4 minutes. Once they do, flip them gently but swiftly with a spatula and continue to cook until they have completely inflated, a minute or two. Remove them from the oven (don't turn it off) and immediately cover them with a clean cloth. Use a pan, round tray, or rolling pin to flatten them, forcing the air out. Let them cool to the touch with the towel still on top.

Use a knife to cut around the edges of each circle to separate it into the 2 thin rounds that separated during the puffing up, and stack them one on top of the other. Try to keep them intact, because it'll be a bit easier to finish the dish that way, but if you don't end up with 2 perfect circles, no matter.

Working in batches, bake the 12 circles on the hot stone once again, turning them over once, until they're crispy and have golden-brown patches here and there, 1 to 1½ minutes per batch. Let them cool completely.

Generously butter one side of each of the crispy disks (a pastry brush makes this easy). Sprinkle the bottarga over 6 of the disks. Sprinkle a little salt and crumbled chili over each one, then drizzle with the tiniest bit of olive oil. Make 6 sandwiches, topping the bottarga with the remaining disks, butter side down.

Gently break each one in half and eat straightaway.

MOZZARELLA AND SPECK SANDWICHES

This is a great sandwich when you've got a drink in one hand and want a nibble in the other. Unlike most grilled cheese, this little guy doesn't require a slathering of butter to go perfectly crispy. I like to use day-old good bread, the airy kind pocked with holes. I squish the sandwiches with my spatula as they cook, and the fat from the mozzarella leaks out and urges the bread toward golden brown. Once you've made this a few times, you can start playing around a bit, tucking in herbs like basil or rosemary.   **serves 4 as lunch, 8 as a snack**

Two ½-pound balls mozzarella di bufala
Eight ½-inch-thick slices day-old rustic bread
16 thin slices speck or 8 thin slices prosciutto

Drain the mozzarella and cut it into sixteen ¼-inch-thick slices. Lay the slices on a few layers of paper towels and pat them with more paper towels, pressing on the slices a bit to sop up some of their liquid.

Put 2 slices of mozzarella on each of 4 slices of the bread. Top each with 4 slices of speck or 2 slices of prosciutto (make sure there's plenty hanging off the sides so it can get crispy), then top off with 2 more slices of mozzarella. Top the stacks with the remaining bread and press down lightly.

Grab a large nonstick pan and pop it over medium heat. Once it's nice and hot, place 2 of the sandwiches in the pan. Every now and again, give the sandwiches a good old press with the back of a spatula. Once their bottom sides are golden with patches of brown here and there, about 6 minutes, carefully flip the sandwiches. Cook on their other sides, again making sure to give the sandwiches a few good squishes, until they're deep golden brown, about 6 minutes more. Repeat with the remaining sandwiches and serve.

big bowls of soup

GREEN PEA AND HAM SOUP

I've eaten split pea and ham soup for as long as I can remember. On chilly days when my dad was being stingy with the heat, it especially hit the spot. But this concept is just as good in the springtime, when sugary fresh peas show up at the greenmarket. Although I must admit that I rarely feel like shelling peas at home after a long day in the kitchen, and I love frozen peas, which are consistently fine, so that's what I call for here. The finished dish is bright green and sweet, with little chunks of ham, carrots, and cool white blobs of crème fraîche floating on its surface. **serves 4**

FOR THE BROTH

2 pounds meaty smoked ham hocks

½ medium Spanish onion, halved

3 small celery stalks, very roughly chopped

½ medium carrot, peeled, very roughly chopped

1 head garlic, halved horizontally, not peeled

1 fresh bay leaf, or ½ dried

6 black peppercorns

FOR THE SOUP

4 tablespoons unsalted butter

½ small Spanish onion, finely chopped

1 small carrot, peeled and cut into ½-inch pieces

2 teaspoons Maldon or another flaky sea salt

½ cup dry white wine, such as Sauvignon Blanc

Five-fingered pinch of mint leaves, plus some torn leaves for finishing

Two 10-ounce packages Birds Eye frozen baby peas

Extra virgin olive oil

Freshly ground black pepper

3 or 4 tablespoons crème fraîche

Make the broth: Combine the hocks, vegetables, bay leaf, peppercorns, and 8 cups of water in a medium stockpot and bring to a boil over high heat. Turn the heat to low, put the lid on, and cook at a nice steady simmer until the meat on the hocks is so tender it's almost falling off the bone, 4 to 5 hours.

Carefully remove the hocks and put them in a big bowl. Strain the cooking liquid through a sieve into the bowl, and discard the vegetables and aromatics. Let the hocks cool in the liquid.

When the hocks are cool enough to handle, pull off the meat in bite-sized chunks. Discard the bones and any hard bits and some of the fat, but don't throw away the skin—I add the skin to the soup in thin slices, along with the chunks of ham. You don't *have* to, but I like the way it goes sticky in the soup. You can keep the stock and meat (moistened with a splash of stock) in separate airtight containers in the fridge for up to two days. Gently warm the meat and skin before proceeding with the recipe. This recipe requires only 4 cups of stock—you may freeze the leftover stock for up to a month for your next batch of soup.

Make the soup: Put the butter in a large pot that has a lid and set it over medium heat. Once the butter starts to froth, add the onion, carrot, and salt and stir. Cover the pot and cook, stirring every now and again, until the onions are soft and creamy (but not colored) and the carrots are tender but firm, about 15 minutes.

Add the wine and bring it to a boil (turn the heat up if you need to). Let the wine boil until it's all but gone, about 5 minutes. Add the mint and 4 cups of the ham broth and bring the liquid to a boil, then add the peas. (At this point, the carrots will have bobbed to the top. I like to pick out most of the carrot chunks before pureeing the soup, then add them back after. That way, you can nibble on them in the soup, getting that bit of texture.) Cook at a simmer until the peas are warmed through and tender, about 5 minutes.

Blend the pot's contents, in batches, until smooth. Return all the bright-green pea puree to the large pot, add the ham pieces and carrots, and cook at a very gentle simmer for about

5 minutes, just to let the flavors mingle and heat the ham. Have a taste, and season with salt. How much you need to add will depend on how salty the ham hocks are.

Add a generous drizzle of olive oil, several twists of black pepper, and the torn mint leaves. Then add the crème fraîche in little blobs here and there, so everyone will get a bit. Serve the soup in the pot, with small bowls alongside.

IT ISN'T EASY BEING GREEN

I love to let the ingredients in this soup mingle in the pot for a few hours so the flavors marry. Doing this, however, sacrifices the soup's lovely bright green color for a pondy, murky one. I don't mind the color change, but some people might. If you'd like to make the soup the night before and want it to stay bright, set up a big bowl of ice water and set another big bowl inside. Once the soup is done, pour it into the bowl and stir until it's cold.

SPRING SOUP

This is soup of a moment—of the first warm days of the year, of cool breezes and blossoming trees. It takes advantage of the last of the season's Jerusalem artichokes, which won't come around again until fall. And it is a lovely way to use the pretty young onions and garlic piled up on the tables at the farmers' market. These three vegetables, along with carrots, form the base of the soup. You cook the vegetables just until their sweetness begins to show itself but not so much that it will obscure the other spring goodies you plunk in as the soup cooks. I use baby artichokes, asparagus, and ramps, but you can use any seasonal veg you'd like. Perhaps you'll decide on sweet peas instead of artichokes, or end-of-season broccoli rabe instead of ramps. **serves 4**

5 tablespoons extra virgin olive oil

4 pinkie-thin young spring garlic stalks, roots and all but an inch
of the green stalk trimmed, very thinly sliced

About a dozen bulbous spring onions (or a dozen small shallots),
trimmed of stalks and leaves and cut into small wedges

About 5 teaspoons Maldon or another flaky sea salt

About 10 small Jerusalem artichokes, peeled
and kept in a bowl of water

1 medium carrot, peeled and chopped into ½-inch pieces

4 small baby artichokes, trimmed
(see How to Prep Artichokes, page 61)

⅔ cup cooked white beans, such as flageolets,
with their cooking liquid

5 tablespoons heavy cream

A small bunch of ramps, separated into leaves and bulbs
with an inch of stem (see Cleaning Ramps, page 43)

A small handful of mint leaves, like black mint or spearmint

A small handful of opal or regular basil leaves

About 1 dozen pencil-thin asparagus spears, woody bottoms discarded,
stalks thinly sliced, and tips reserved

Combine the olive oil, spring garlic, spring onions or shallots, and 4 teaspoons of the salt in a 4- to 6-quart pot and set over medium-high heat. Once you hear the mixture sizzle, turn the heat down to medium-low. Cook, stirring occasionally, until the spring garlic and onions are translucent but not colored, about 12 minutes.

Drain the Jerusalem artichokes, pat dry, and chop into bite-sized pieces.

Turn the heat up to medium-high, add the carrots and Jerusalem artichokes to the pot, and cook just until the Jerusalem artichokes start to turn translucent, about 4 minutes. Measure the bean liquid and add enough water to give you 4 cups total. Add the mixture to the vegetables. Let the liquid come to a bare simmer, and tweak the heat to maintain it for 10 minutes.

Add the artichokes, beans, and heavy cream and keep cooking at a bare simmer (though it'll get a bit more rapid as the liquid cooks down) until the artichokes are tender (they're ready when you can easily poke one through the thickest part with the tip of a spoon), about 30 minutes more.

As the soup simmers, halve any large ramp bulbs lengthwise. Toss the mint, basil, and ramp leaves together and finely chop them.

Once the artichokes are tender, add the asparagus tips and ramp bulbs and stems to the pot. Wait a minute or so, then add the thinly sliced asparagus and the ramp leaves, mint, and basil and cook at a gentle simmer until the asparagus is tender but still a bit crunchy, about 2 minutes.

Take the pot off the heat. Scoop about 1 cup of the soup, both liquid and some chunks, into a blender and blend until smooth and creamy. Stir the puree back into the pot, along with the remaining teaspoon of salt, or more to your taste, and serve.

HOW TO PREP ARTICHOKES

Fill a good-sized bowl with water and squeeze in enough lemon juice to make the water taste acidic. Working with one artichoke at a time, pull off the green outer leaves until only the soft yellowish leaves are left. Cut off about ½ inch of the stem, and cut off about 1 inch from the tip of the artichoke. Trim off any tough green stuff at the base of the artichoke, gently peel the outer layer from the stem, and drop it in the lemon water (to prevent discoloration). Halve the artichokes lengthwise, scoop out the feathery choke, and submerge the halves again in the water. Dry the artichokes before you use them.

SEVEN-VEGETABLE SOUP

This is the sort of soup version of bubble and squeak. The first time I made it, I used the veg I had left over from Christmas dinner, and it had the same magic as great bubble—the vegetables developed a heavenly togetherness but still retained their individual tastes and textures. Then one day, I re-created it using all fresh stuff. (Back then, I may have called it five-vegetable soup, but it seems like every year I make it, I add more vegetables.) It's a great one to save for a rainy day or to pack in a thermos when you go apple picking, especially alongside some lovely pork sandwiches.

serves 4

¼ cup extra virgin olive oil, plus a few glugs

1 large Spanish onion, chopped

2 tablespoons Maldon or another flaky sea salt

1 grapefruit-sized celeriac, peeled and cut into ¾-inch pieces

1 medium fennel bulb, rough outer layer removed and root end trimmed, cut into ¾-inch pieces

4 medium Jerusalem artichokes, peeled and cut into ¾-inch pieces

2 medium Yukon Gold potatoes, peeled, rinsed (see Potatoes, page 10), and cut into ¾-inch pieces

1 medium carrot, peeled and cut into ¾-inch pieces

1 tennis ball–sized turnip or rutabaga, peeled and cut into ¾-inch pieces

2 medium parsnips, peeled and cut into ¾-inch pieces

3 cups Chicken Stock (see Note, page 302)

1 teaspoon finely chopped rosemary

2 to 3 dried pequin chilies or pinches of red pepper flakes (optional)

1 lemon, halved (optional)

Warm a 6- to 8-quart soup pot over medium-low heat for a minute or two, then add the ¼ cup olive oil, the onions, and salt. Give a stir, cover the pot, and cook, stirring occasionally, until the onions are very soft and creamy (you don't want any color on them), about 15 minutes.

Add the rest of the vegetables, stir, cover the pot again, and let them cook gently, stirring rather roughly now and then, for 25 or 30 minutes; the vegetables should still hold their shape but be beginning to soften. Add the stock, bring it to a gentle simmer, and cook, uncovered, stirring and mushing the vegetables a bit, until all the vegetables are tender, anywhere from 15 to 30 minutes.

Add a few glugs of olive oil and the rosemary. Crumble in the chilies, if you're using them. Have a taste, and add a little more salt, if you'd like, and a few squeezes of lemon, if you feel it needs to be a bit brighter. Serve while it's still steamy.

Note: The key to this simple soup is in the preparation. I chop the celeriac, fennel, Jerusalem artichokes, potatoes, carrot, turnip, and parsnips into oblique pieces (see Cutting Vegetables, page 7), so the chunky parts keep their shape and the thinner edges crumble off and thicken the soup.

big bowls of soup

SUMMER TOMATO SOUP

Summertime in a bowl, this is. I make it when I've got a bunch of juicy heirloom tomatoes so heavy they're almost bursting. Really nice ripe tomatoes are especially important here, because there's not much else to the soup beyond a little garlic, basil, and olive oil. If I served it at the restaurant, I might add some butter or crème fraîche—goat cheese might be nice, too, wouldn't it?—but even without that extra dose of fat, when you whiz the tomatoes together in the blender, all of a sudden they turn creamy, because of the olive oil and the air introduced by blending. I love that. I often eat the soup warm, though it's quite good cold, as long as you season it with just a bit more salt.   **serves 4**

7 medium heirloom tomatoes (about 3 pounds)—
a mix of several varieties is nice

¼ cup plus 3 tablespoons extra virgin olive oil

5 garlic cloves, sliced

A small handful of basil leaves

3 tablespoons Maldon or another flaky sea salt

Halve the tomatoes through the stem and cut out the cores and any hard, pale bits. Use your fingers to push out the juice and seeds, strain the juice through a sieve into a bowl, stirring and smooshing to extract as much liquid as possible, and discard the solids left behind.

Combine 3 tablespoons of the olive oil and the garlic in a medium pot or deep pan that has a lid and is large enough to hold the tomatoes comfortably, then set it over medium-high heat. Once the garlic begins to sizzle, cook it, stirring often, until it's a light golden color and fragrant, a minute or two.

Add the tomatoes and the strained juice along with 5 or so of the basil leaves and 1 tablespoon of the salt, and give a little stir. After a minute or so, pour in ¼ cup water. Turn the heat to low and cover the pot. Peek inside the pot after 5 minutes or so, and when the tomatoes look like they're swimming in their own juice, take off the lid and adjust the heat so you get a nice gentle simmer. Let simmer, uncovered, for about 20 minutes, stirring occasionally and breaking up the tomatoes slightly so they release more juice, until the liquid has thickened a bit.

Turn off the heat and add the remaining 2 tablespoons salt, the rest of the basil, and the remaining ¼ cup olive oil. Blend the mixture, working in batches if necessary, until it's very smooth and has a lovely creamy texture. Pour it back into the pot, stir, and add a bit more salt, if you'd like. Serve in bowls.

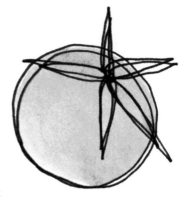

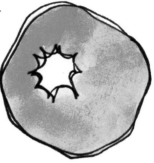

SMOKED HADDOCK CHOWDER

We've been serving this chowder at The Pig since the beginning. It's the kind of thing you'd see in England at a country pub or a fishing village eatery. At The Pig, we dice the vegetables into tiny cubes, but at home, I prefer to keep the veg in rustic pieces. The soup still has the same flavor, and I like chomping on the odd piece of carrot and celery. Once you bring out the sweetness in the vegetables, you combine them with a mixture of milk and cream infused with the flavor of smoked haddock (you might spot it sold as "finnan haddie," as it's called in the U.K.). A little heat from chili and brightness from lemon and herbs bring relief from all that richness, urging you to have yet another spoonful.   **serves 4**

2 cups heavy cream

2 cups whole milk

¾ pound Yukon Gold or russet (baking) potatoes, peeled, rinsed
(see Potatoes, page 10), and cut into ½-inch pieces

½ pound skin-on smoked haddock (defrosted if frozen)

¼ cup extra virgin olive oil, plus a few glugs for finishing

3 ounces skinned smoked slab bacon, cut into 1- by ¼-inch pieces

1 large carrot, peeled and cut into ¾-inch pieces

2 medium celery stalks, cut into ¾-inch pieces,
plus ¼ cup roughly chopped celery leaves

1 large Spanish onion, cut into ¾-inch pieces

Maldon or another flaky sea salt

½ cup dry white wine, such as Sauvignon Blanc

2 dried pequin chilies, crumbled, or pinches of red pepper flakes

2 cups Fish Stock (see recipe, page 304), or a little more as needed

A small handful of roughly chopped flat-leaf parsley leaves

1 lemon, halved

Combine the cream and milk in a medium pot, add the potatoes, and bring to a boil over medium-high heat. Turn the heat down and simmer until the potatoes are tender enough to crush easily between your fingers but still hold their form, 15 to 20 minutes. Remove the pot from the heat, add the haddock, and let it steep.

Meanwhile, heat ¼ cup of the olive oil in a large pot over medium heat. When the oil barely begins to smoke, add the bacon and cook until some of the fat has rendered and the bacon has just a bit of color, about 2 minutes. Add the carrot, celery, onion, and ½ teaspoon salt and cook, stirring every now and again, for about 8 minutes, checking occasionally to make sure all the vegetables are happy.

Add the wine and crumble in the chilies, stir, and cook until the wine evaporates, stirring to get the sticky bits up. It'll all look a bit creamy. Add the stock and let it simmer until it has reduced by half. Turn off the heat.

Remove (and reserve) the haddock, and spoon out half the potatoes and cream mixture into a blender. Blend until smooth, then add this along with the remaining cream mixture to the pot with the vegetables. Turn the heat to medium and bring to a simmer.

Meanwhile, pull off and discard the skin from the haddock. Run your fingers along the flesh, picking out any little bones. With your hands, pull the flesh into bite-sized pieces, and add them to the soup. Cook on low for 5 more minutes.

Pour in a few glugs of olive oil and add half of the celery and parsley leaves, along with a good squeeze of lemon. Take the pot off the heat, stir, and give the chowder a taste. Maybe you you'd like another teaspoon of salt or a few more chilies, or a bit more lemon juice to add brightness. If it's thicker than you like it, add a little water or more fish stock, then taste it and tweak the flavors again.

Ladle the chowder into bowls and top each one with some of the remaining celery and parsley leaves and a drizzle of olive oil. Serve straightaway.

well-dressed greens and things

chef

After I graduated from cooking school, I needed a job. My sister had an in at a restaurant in London called Kensington Place. It was one of the restaurants leading the way in the British culinary revival. At the time, the chef was a guy named Rowley Leigh.

My interview was odd. He and I sat at a table just by the restaurant's revolving doors. I asked if he wanted to see my résumé. He said no. At first I thought that might be a bad sign. But it was probably for the best, as my résumé was more or less nonexistent. We chatted a bit, and during a lull in our conversation, I asked what was in the little bowls on each table. They looked like olives with long stems. Caperberries, he said. I asked if I could try one. I think my curiosity swayed him, because right after I popped one in my mouth, he said I could have the job.

Really intelligent and tremendously skilled, he had an interesting teaching style. A few hours before service, he'd write down a few specials. Sometimes he'd explain rather vaguely how he wanted the dishes executed and other times he didn't bother at all. He certainly never provided a recipe. He'd disappear from the kitchen and when he returned twenty minutes later, you'd be in the shit. He'd have a look around and say, "What, you're not done with your specials yet?" then finish them all in five minutes. He'd let you struggle and freak out a little, then swoop in and save the day.

After service, I was always sweaty and hungry. I worked thirteen-hour days, always tasting but never eating anything, determined to prove my devotion and skill. At the end of my shift, I'd often take some leftover cotecchino, slice it into big chunks, and put it between slices of crusty bread. To this day, whenever I come across that lip-smacking, sticky sausage, I think of Rowley. This may be the first time I've called him by name and not "Chef"—after all, he was my first.

At Kensington Place, I learned how to cook consistently, how to make everything look and taste the same each time I made it. All that repetition might sound dull, but it created my foundation. If you don't cook something again and again, then how can you learn from it? The first several times you cook a dish, you'll probably make some mistakes—maybe you'll rush the browning and fail to develop an ingredient's sweetness, or maybe you'll freak out because the braise that took two hours the other day is taking double that today. But mistakes are a good thing, actually, as long as you learn from them. (Although it might shock my kitchen staff to hear me say so.)

CAESAR SALAD

I grew up eating boring salads, horrible and underdressed. The old-school salads I learned to make at culinary school, like Waldorf and Niçoise and the mayo-and-curry-spiked Coronation Chicken, were better, for sure. But the Caesar was the first salad I ever really loved. Soon after I graduated, I got a job at a restaurant called Kensington Place. Rowley Leigh, the chef, would mound plain Gem lettuce on a plate and serve it with Caesar dressing on the side. Oh, that dressing! Not only was the flavor a tangy, umami-packed thrill, but it was also very "clean," as we chefs sometimes say. That is, you could taste the individual components—first to register was the saltiness, not necessarily the fishiness, of the anchovies, then came the Parm and garlic, and finally, the tang of the vinegar.

Because of my early bland salad experiences, I like mine extra punchy, even, in this case, what some people might consider a little overdressed. Romaine is quite watery and it needs the dressing to cut through that flatness. This is a salad I like to make and eat with my hands. I rub the dressing onto each leaf, each one like a little canoe. I'm especially fond of the freshly-baked-bread taste of the croutons, which makes you want to seek out another, and then another, and the refreshing quality you get from serving the salad chilled. Eat it quickly, before it warms up. **serves 4**

7 whole salt-packed anchovies, rinsed, soaked, and filleted
(see Filleting Salt-Packed Anchovies, page 10)
2 medium garlic cloves, smashed and peeled
3 tablespoons Dijon mustard
¼ cup champagne vinegar
1 large egg
1 cup sunflower, peanut, or grapeseed oil
A 1-ounce chunk of Parmesan, very finely grated

2 heads Romaine lettuce, chilled
Croutons (see Croutons, page 12)
A chunk of Parmesan for grating
Maldon or another flaky sea salt
A few anchovy fillets for garnish

well-dressed greens and things

Put the anchovy fillets and garlic in a small food processor and pulse to a rough paste. Add the mustard and vinegar, crack in the egg, and blend until the mixture is smooth and creamy. With the processor on, gradually drizzle in the oil in a steady stream. Finally, add the Parmesan and blend until it's all well combined. Scrape the dressing into a bowl, cover it with plastic wrap, then pop it into the fridge to chill and thicken up. (It'll keep for up to 3 days.)

Trim the root ends of the Romaine heads and discard the large, floppy outer leaves. Separate the remaining leaves and put them in a very large mixing bowl. Refrigerate the leaves until they are nice and cold. Pour in about ½ cup of the dressing. I like to use my fingers to gently rub this dressing onto both sides of the leaves, so you get a little bit everywhere. Gradually add more dressing, just until it's all nicely coated. Be nimble and fast like a salad ninja, because you don't want your hands to warm up the lettuce and dressing. Add the croutons and toss a few times so they get a touch of the dressing. Then add a little more dressing if you need to. (I usually end up using about half the dressing and saving the rest in the fridge for another day.)

Layer the leaves of the salad, so they face this way and that and so they're not all in a clump, on a platter and scatter the croutons here and there. Garnish with the anchovies. Grate some Parmesan on top, taste, and add a little salt, if you'd like. Eat it immediately—with your hands.

LENTIL AND CHICKPEA SALAD
WITH FETA AND TAHINI

This salad is a delightful jumble of different textures and flavors: there's the sweet crunch of red onion, the salty feta, and the creamy, lemony dressing coating the delicate little lentils and hearty chickpeas. It's completely vegetarian, and yet somehow, when I take a bite, the cumin, the funky cheese, and the sesame seeds all conspire to create a flavor that I swear reminds me of roasted lamb. Sometimes I serve it alongside grilled merguez sausages or a nice rack of lamb, but I'll also turn it into a meal with a bowl of fleshy Marinated Roasted Peppers (see recipe, page 216).   **serves 4 to 6**

FOR THE LENTILS

Scant 1 cup dried Puy or Casteluccio lentils, rinsed and picked over

2 large garlic cloves, halved lengthwise

2 sage sprigs

2 tablespoons extra virgin olive oil

FOR THE DRESSING AND SALAD

2 teaspoons coriander seeds, toasted and ground
(see Spices, page 9)

1 teaspoon cumin seeds, toasted and ground
(see Spices, page 9)

½ large garlic clove

Maldon or another flaky sea salt

2 tablespoons well-stirred tahini paste

About ¼ cup freshly squeezed lemon juice

2 tablespoons plus 2 teaspoons extra virgin olive oil

1¾ cups drained chickpeas, low-sodium canned or
Simple Chickpeas (see recipe, page 250)

½ small preserved lemon, pith and flesh discarded, rind finely diced

1 very small red onion, thinly sliced into half moons

A handful of small, delicate cilantro sprigs

A scant ¼ pound feta, preferably goat's-milk

1½ tablespoons raw sesame seeds, toasted in a dry pan
until a shade or two darker

Make the lentils: Put the lentils, garlic, sage, and olive oil in a small pot, along with 2 cups cold water, and set it over medium heat. Let the water come to a simmer (don't let it boil), then turn the heat to low and cook the lentils at a very gentle simmer just until they're tender—no longer gritty or mealy, but still with some texture to them—about 25 minutes. Take the pan off the heat and let the lentils cool. They'll continue to cook a bit as they do.

Once the lentils are cool, drain them very well and pick out and discard the sage and garlic. You'll have about 2 cups of cooked lentils.

Make the dressing: Mix together the ground coriander and cumin in a small bowl.

Mash the garlic clove to a paste with 1 teaspoon salt in a mortar. (Or use a large knife to chop and mash them to a paste on the cutting board.) Combine the mashed garlic, the tahini paste, 3 tablespoons of the lemon juice, 2 tablespoons of the olive oil, 1 teaspoon of the ground spice mixture, and 2 tablespoons water in a bowl. Stir the mixture well. Have a taste and consider adding another teaspoon of lemon juice.

Assemble the salad: Toss the lentils with the drained chickpeas, preserved lemon rind, and 1 teaspoon salt in a large mixing bowl. Pour in the tahini dressing and toss it all together really well.

Put the onion slices in a medium bowl and break them up with your fingers. Sprinkle in 2 good pinches of salt, then add 2 teaspoons of the lemon juice. Add the remaining 2 teaspoons olive oil and the cilantro and toss gently but well with your hands. Crumble in the cheese; I like to keep some of it in large bite-sized chunks. Give another gentle toss.

Scatter a few handfuls of the chickpea-lentil mixture onto a large platter in one layer. Scrape the onion and cheese mixture into the bowl with the rest of the lentils and chickpeas and toss it gently so the ingredients are well distributed but the cilantro stays pert. Scatter this mixture on top of the lentils and chickpeas on the platter. I make sure to pluck out a few of the cilantro sprigs and put them on top. Sprinkle on some of the remaining spice mixture and then the sesame seeds and serve.

Note:
You can cook the chickpeas and lentils the day before. Store them separately, covered, in the fridge and let them come to room temperature before you make the salad.

a good salad

I make salads with my hands. I like to touch food, to know it and control it. That might mean crushing some things between my fingers, massaging Romaine with sturdy dressing, or arranging ingredients to make sure they're not sitting in a big lump on the plate.

As I get older, I find that it's quite nice to have a simple salad, though that doesn't mean plain old lettuce leaves with vinaigrette. I can't bear being bored: I want something that keeps my interest with contrasting flavors, textures, and temperatures. There are no rules to salad. It can be warm or cold or both. Lettuce is an option, not a must. Whether you're making pumpkin salad in the winter or tossing spring peas with mint and pecorino, whatever is in a salad has to be tasty. Otherwise, there's no point in making it. Try to understand each component—smell it, touch it, taste it. A tomato today might not be as sweet or tart or firm as the one you had a few weeks back.

Some salads are about one star ingredient. If they are, you want to be able to taste that ingredient most of all. Other components are just there in service of it. Then there are salads that are about the interplay of a variety of ingredients. Either way, every ingredient matters—for instance, I just couldn't imagine Carrot, Avocado, and Orange Salad (see recipe, page 88) without cilantro, or Radish Salad (see recipe, page 82) without basil—and no one should overpower another.

And I never just dump it all in a bowl and serve it. It's nice to arrange the ingredients on a plate so there will be a good mix of flavors and textures in each bite. Proportions are important too. No one should have to root around in his or her salad, lettuce flying, trying to find an almond. Yet, on the other hand, while it's nice to give people what they want in each bite, it's also nice to hold back a little. If they have to search a little to find another almond, they'll get that joy when they hit one.

I love a well-seasoned, well-dressed salad. The dressing has to be vibrant and balanced. It can't be bland, because once you add it to your lettuces (which are mostly made up of water) or other components, it'll taste less intense. And please, gently but thoroughly dry your ingredients—otherwise, even a fantastic dressing will slip right off. Finally, dress your sturdy ingredients first, and gently toss everything together with the delicates right before you serve the salad.

RADISH SALAD

This salad is a hands-on endeavor made with what my mate Fergus Henderson would call "the claw." The first time I met him—not in England, where we're both from, but at The Pig, when we threw a party to celebrate the launch of one of his cookbooks— he popped into the kitchen for a chat. That's when I noticed that he touches salads the way I touch salads. I watched him stick his hands into a bowl and start smoosh-ing and bruising things to get all the flavors to come together. Right then, I knew we'd get on well: "the claw" is something I do too.

You get in there with your hands and squeeze the Parmesan, basil, and salt against the radishes. Then you add the olive oil and lemon until it's all really bright. The aim is to mush the cheese just enough that some of it goes creamy and thickens the dressing while the rest holds its shape, little nuggets of salty sharpness. And it might seem odd, but the salad just doesn't quite work without both the Parmesan and the basil.

serves 4

1 pound radishes (about 25), topped, tailed, cut into large
bite-sized pieces, and chilled (see A Note on Radishes, page 83)

A small handful of basil leaves

Maldon or another flaky sea salt

A 2½-ounce chunk of Parmesan, cut into slices,
some thick and some thin

2 tablespoons freshly squeezed lemon juice, or to taste

3 tablespoons extra virgin olive oil

2 small handfuls radish sprouts or arugula

Just before you'd like to serve the salad, combine the radishes, basil, and 3 healthy pinches of salt in a big bowl. Grab a handful of the mixture at a time and smoosh the basil and salt against the radishes for about 30 seconds to release the basil's aromatic oils. Add the cheese and go at the radishes again until some of the cheese goes creamy, some is in little chunks, and some is still in larger dime-sized chunks.

Add the lemon juice and olive oil and toss well. Give it a taste, and add an-other pinch or two of salt if you'd like. Maybe some more lemon, too, but keep in mind that although you want the salad to taste acidic and bright, the lemon shouldn't dominate. Add the sprouts or arugula and toss gently but thoroughly. Scatter the salad on a large plate or platter (not in a bowl, please) and serve.

A NOTE ON RADISHES

Your task is finding fresh, firm, spicy radishes. Spongy or watery ones won't cut it. Taste your radishes. If they're crisp but missing a bit of heat, you can add a pinch or two of dried chili when you make the salad. I love to use a mixture of French Breakfast, Icicle, Watermelon, and Easter Egg radishes, because it's nice to have the different sizes and colors. Of course, you can use one type and be done with it.

Wash them well and scrape off any gnarly bits with your knife. But they're tough little things that grow in the ground, so don't fret over a few nicks. Cut them in a way that shows off their shape. For example, I love halving long, thin radishes lengthwise. Leave on a bit of the green top for the color and texture. If you're very lucky and find radishes with pert, lovely greens, don't remove the greens. Just trim off any brown or wilted bits.

FRIED PIG'S EAR SALAD

This is my homage to Fergus Henderson, a friend and a chef I've learned so much from. His food is simple but succeeds because of the little details. I remember having a lovely shrimp and white cabbage salad at St. John, one of his restaurants in London. What really got me was how it had just enough chervil to make you wonder, "What is that herb?" Fergus thinks about that kind of thing, how to cook food that makes you wonder. In his first cookbook, *The Whole Beast,* he writes that for his signature bone marrow with parsley salad, there should be just enough capers so you end up searching for them, like the raisins in raisin bran. I love that. It might sound like a small thing, but it's the difference between giving people what they *think* they want and giving them what will be truly amazing.

He loves using stuff like capers and lemon to give you relief when you're tucking into something fatty like pig's ear, which is crunchy and sort of sticks to your teeth like peanut butter. In this salad, the dressing, with the intense pops of tartness from the lemon segments, makes you want to eat more pig's ear, and its salty cartilage and fat makes you crave more dressing.

I love eating the salad chilled—the greens *and* dressing—which makes it refreshing despite that fried cartilage and fat. Using whole ears adds a bit of fun, though that might be too much for some. You can always cut the ears into long strips while they're cold, then fry them the same way.

serves 4

4 pig's ears (about 3 ounces each)
About 6 cups rendered duck fat, gently warmed until liquid
2 medium Belgian endives
1 medium head Treviso, radicchio, or two red endives
Peanut oil for deep-frying
Kosher salt
Lemon Caper Dressing (see recipe, page 284), chilled
A small handful of arugula

Special Equipment
Deep fryer with a lid; parchment paper

Preheat the oven to 250°F.

Make sure your pig's ears are free of hair. Remove any that you spot with a sharp knife or razor. Put the ears in an ovenproof saucepan with a lid that holds them snugly, then add enough duck fat to cover them. Cut out a circle of parchment paper that'll cover the ears, put it on top of them, and top it with a saucer to weigh them down. Cover the pan, put it in the oven, and cook just until the ears are so tender that when you give them a firm pinch, your fingers meet, about 4 hours.

Remove the ears from the oven and let them cool submerged in the fat. Once the ears are cool, remove them from the fat, wipe them off, and pat them dry. (Strain and reserve the duck fat for another use.)

Meanwhile, separate the leaves of the endives and Treviso or radicchio. Put them in a large bowl, cover with plastic wrap, and put the bowl in the fridge. (I love the contrast between the cool leaves and the hot pig's ear.)

Pour the peanut oil into a deep fryer and heat to 350°F. (The amount of oil will depend on your fryer's capacity.) I don't recommend doing this in a fryer without a lid, because the oil will pop, spit, and spatter like mad. Try not to be alarmed. Gently add 1 ear (or 2 if you have a larger fryer), immediately close the lid, and fry until deliciously golden brown, about 8 minutes. Transfer to paper towels to drain and season right away on both sides with salt. Keep the ear(s) somewhere warm, like a toasty spot near the stove, while you fry the rest.

Take the bowl of endive from the fridge. Sprinkle 5 tablespoons or so of the chilled dressing over the leaves, making sure it gets into all the curves. Add the arugula and mix gently but thoroughly with your fingers, so the lemon segments in the dressing stay more or less whole but every leaf gets some dressing.

Put the greens on a platter, top it off with the warm, crispy ears, and add a little more dressing, if you fancy.

Note: All recipes should be cooked with care, but that's especially true in this case, because you're frying in hot fat. Fortunately, nowadays you can buy affordable fryers with thermostats and lids, which makes things much easier. I strongly suggest you invest in a fryer with a lid, whether you mean to make this recipe or you're just a fan of frying.

CARROT, AVOCADO, AND ORANGE SALAD

This is my Six Degrees of Kevin Bacon salad. The two main ingredients—carrot and avocado—might not seem compatible or connected, but your first bite will convince you otherwise. The carrots are roasted with cumin and paired with orange, both classic pairings for the vegetable. The citrus goes great with cilantro, and both are a fine match for avocado. Before you know it, you have this fresh, vibrant salad. I love the carrots roasted to the same creamy softness of avocado. The contrast comes not from the texture but from the fact that one's warm from the oven and the other's cool from the fridge.

Sorry if I got your hopes up, but despite the salad's nickname, there's no bacon.

serves 4

4 medium garlic cloves, smashed and peeled

Maldon or another flaky sea salt

1½ teaspoons cumin seeds, toasted and ground (see Spices, page 9)

1½ teaspoons coriander seeds, toasted and ground (see Spices, page 9)

1 to 1½ teaspoons crumbled dried pequin chilies or red pepper flakes

¼ cup plus 2 tablespoons extra virgin olive oil

30 or so similarly sized (each about the size of your pointer finger) young carrots, not peeled, ½ inch of the green tops left on

3 tennis-ball-sized oranges

3 ripe Hass avocados, chilled

2 tablespoons freshly squeezed lemon juice

A handful of small, delicate cilantro sprigs

Preheat the oven to 400°F.

Pound the garlic with a healthy pinch of salt in a mortar until you have a wet, fairly smooth paste. (You can also do this on a cutting board, chopping and mashing and chopping and mashing until you're satisfied.) Put the paste in a large mixing bowl. Add the cumin, coriander, chilies, and ¼ cup of the olive oil and stir well, then add the carrots and toss well so they're coated with the oil and spices. Sprinkle on 3 healthy pinches of salt, crushing the grains with your fingers as you add them, and toss again.

Put the carrots in a large shallow baking dish in one layer. Scrape out the extra garlic, spices, and oil from the bowl and spread evenly on top of the carrots. Pour ¼ cup water into an empty spot in the casserole (you don't want to wash off the tasty oily stuff) and tilt the dish so the water spreads across the bottom.

Cover the dish tightly with foil and put it in the oven. Cook the carrots for 25 minutes. Take off the foil and keep cooking until the carrots are lightly browned, and about as tender and creamy as avocado flesh, but not so soft that they threaten to fall apart, about 35 minutes more.

While the carrots are roasting, segment the orange as you would a lemon (see Segmenting Lemons, page 284). Squeeze the membranes into a small bowl to release the juice. Set it aside.

When the carrots are done, take the dish out of the oven and let it sit until the carrots have cooled a bit but are still warm.

Meanwhile, take the avocados from the fridge. Halve them lengthwise, remove the pits, and peel the halves. Cut the flesh lengthwise into slices about the same size as the carrots—the slices should be sturdy enough that they don't break up when you toss them.

Put the avocado slices in a large mixing bowl and add the reserved orange juice, the lemon juice, the remaining 2 tablespoons olive oil, and a healthy pinch or two of salt. Toss gently and well with your hands. Push the avocado to one side of the bowl. Add the carrots a handful at a time, scraping and tossing them in the beautiful green liquid in the bowl before adding the next handful. Make sure to scrape out and add all the garlicky spices left in the baking dish. Toss it all together gently, being careful not to break the avocado slices.

Stack the carrots, avocado, and orange segments on a platter or in a serving bowl so they're facing this way and that. Top with the cilantro and serve right away.

ESCAROLE SALAD WITH ROQUEFORT, PEARS, AND WALNUTS

Yet another salad I love to eat nice and cold. The chill makes it especially refreshing and palate cleansing. The escarole is the crisp and slightly bitter backdrop for the creamy, salty blue cheese, but there's just enough of it so it doesn't overpower the aromatic, floral pear. You could actually skip dessert and finish dinner with a small plate of this salad.   **serves 4**

FOR THE WALNUTS

1 packed cup walnuts

A scant ½ cup confectioners' sugar

¼ teaspoon crumbled dried pequin chilies or red pepper flakes

Neutral oil for deep-frying, such as peanut or sunflower

FOR THE SALAD

3 ripe Bartlett pears, chilled

2 heads escarole (about 1¾ pounds total),
outer leaves reserved for another purpose,
pale inner leaves separated and chilled

½ small red onion, cut into 8 thin but not floppy round slices

Roquefort Dressing (see recipe, page 287), chilled

Make the walnuts: Put the walnuts, sugar, and chili in a small pot and add just enough water to cover the walnuts. Set over medium-high heat, bring to a vigorous simmer, and cook until the liquid goes a little syrupy, about 8 minutes. Drain the walnuts.

Wipe out the pot and dry it well. Pour in an inch or two of oil, set the pot over medium-high heat, and let it get just hot enough so that when you add a walnut, it bubbles furiously. Add the walnuts and fry, stirring almost constantly, until they've gone from pale beige-ish brown to golden brown, a minute or two. Use a slotted spoon to transfer them to a few layers of paper towels to drain.

Assemble the salad: Peel, halve, and core the pears, then cut each half into 8 nice pieces.

Make sure the escarole is nice and dry, and put it in a large bowl. Shake on about ¾ cup of the dressing and use your hands to swiftly give each leaf a massage so they all get a nice even coating. Add the pears and give the salad a good but gentle toss, adding a little more dressing if you'd like. Reserve the remaining dressing for another use, such as a dip for vegetables.

Put the salad on a platter or in bowls and disperse the red onion and walnuts over the top, crushing some of the nuts into crumbles.

well-dressed greens and things

BEET AND SMOKED TROUT SALAD

A good dish is often full of contrasts—either in texture, flavor, or temperature, or, as in this case, all three. The warm sweet beets provide heft, something to sink your teeth into. The smoky, earthy trout is salty, tender, and flaky. And then there's the cool crème fraîche to refresh your palate. Make sure to have a little extra crème on hand if you serve the salad on a platter, in case one of your guests nabs it all.

serves 4

3 to 4 bunches medium baby beets (20 to 25), washed well

¼ cup extra virgin olive oil, plus another glug for finishing

2 tablespoons nice, thick balsamic vinegar

Maldon or another flaky sea salt

6 or so skin-on garlic cloves

6 or so thyme sprigs

4 or 5 tablespoons Lemon–Olive Oil Dressing
(see recipe, page 285)

1 pound whole smoked trout (1 or 2)

About 5 tablespoons crème fraîche

¼ cup finely chopped chives

Preheat the oven to 400°F.

Trim the beet stems to about 1 inch, and rinse the beets again. I like to leave the root on because it's quite tender and it makes the salad look rustic. Put the beets in a bowl, drizzle them with the olive oil and balsamic vinegar, sprinkle them with 2 teaspoons salt, and toss well.

Put the beets in a large baking dish. Rather than spreading them in one layer, I like to arrange them in a clump. They not only look great, but, more important, they'll be less likely to burn this way. Drizzle the liquid remaining in the bowl all over the beets. Scatter the garlic cloves and thyme on top of and around the beets. Add ½ cup of water to the pan (don't pour it over the beets, or you'll wash away the seasonings you just added).

Cover the pan tightly with two layers of foil and pop it into the oven. Cook, checking the beets occasionally to be sure there's still liquid in the pan (if there

isn't, add a little more water), just until you can slide a knife into the largest beet without resistance, 50 minutes to an hour, depending on your beets.

Once the beets are tender, remove the foil, give them a gentle stir, and continue roasting, stirring now and then, for about 15 minutes more. You'll hear them sizzling as they cook, and by the time they're done, the skins will be slightly blistered and there won't be any water left in the pan. Once they cool slightly, try one and add a little more salt, if you'd like.

Use a slotted spoon to remove the beets from the pan, leaving any oil behind. If the beets are nice and small (no wider in circumference than a quarter), there's no need to cut them, but halve or quarter any that are larger, popping them into a mixing bowl as you cut them. Stir the dressing well and drizzle about 2 tablespoons of it over the beets. Give the bowl a shake and toss the beets once or twice.

Peel off the skin from the trout. Carefully pull the 2 fillets from the center bone, trying to keep the flesh mostly intact. Gently run your fingers back and forth along the flesh and use your fingers or tweezers to pull out any pin bones you feel.

Break the trout into very large chunks—I like them about the size of my index and middle finger together—and put them in a small mixing bowl. Have a little taste of the trout. Since some smoked trout is saltier than others, you might want to add a little salt. Keep in mind, though, that the dressing you'll add in a second contains some salt too. Drizzle on 2 tablespoons of the dressing, giving the bowl a good shake but being careful not to break up the trout.

Use a slotted spoon to arrange the beets nicely on a large platter or on four plates, and scatter the trout chunks on top and around. Add the crème fraîche in small dollops here and there on top of the beets and trout. Sprinkle the chives all over. Spoon on the liquid remaining in the bowl of beets and a little more olive oil or lemon dressing, if you'd like.

meat
without feet

CHILLED CRAB TRIFLE

My nan was known for the trifles she'd make at Christmas, big, complex sweet treats with layers of custard and lots of cream. One year, she set down one of these massive beauties on the table in front of us, and before we could ooh or aah, the table buckled and broke—and her trifle went flying! The room went quiet, then we all started cracking up. Well, everyone except poor nan. After all, a trifle can be quite time-consuming to make. This savory version—sweet chunks of crab layered with a bright tomato sauce and herby, creamy green goddess dressing—is no exception, assuming you're up for cooking the crab yourself: it will be sweeter and crabbier that way. But if you're short on time, you can substitute a mixture of fresh peekytoe and jumbo lump crabmeat (about a pound and a half total). Just pick it over for any bits of shell that might have been left behind. **serves 6 to 8**

Kosher salt

2 Dungeness crabs (about 2 pounds each), rinsed well

FOR THE TOMATO SAUCE

2 tablespoons extra virgin olive oil

1 medium garlic clove, halved lengthwise

A small handful of basil leaves

1 pound ripe red tomatoes, blanched, peeled, and cored
(see Tomatoes, page 10), then roughly chopped

½ teaspoon Maldon or another flaky sea salt

TO FINISH THE TRIFLE

Green Goddess (see recipe, page 288), chilled

Lemon–Olive Oil Dressing (see recipe, page 285)

2 tablespoons finely chopped chives

Cook the crabs: Bring a pot of water (big enough to hold and cover the crabs) to a boil over high heat. Season the water with salt until it's as salty as the ocean. Make sure the water is at a rapid boil, then submerge the crabs and cover the pot. Once the water comes back to the boil, uncover the pot and cook the crabs for 9 minutes.

While the crabs are cooking, prepare a big bowl of ice water. When the crabs are done, use tongs to plunge them into the ice water. Leave them there until they're fully cold and drain.

Break off the crab legs and claws, then pull off the top shell from each one. Pick out the soft brown meat from the crabs' bodies and set it aside in a bowl. Use a heavy knife to cut each body in half, and use a long flat implement (like the handle of a spoon) to dig out all the meat you can. Add it to the bowl. Finally, use kitchen shears to cut open the legs and claws. Pick out the white meat, trying to keep it as chunky as possible, and put it into the bowl. Cover the bowl with plastic wrap and chill it in the fridge. Save the shells for another purpose, like crab stock.

Make the sauce: Heat the olive oil in a medium saucepan with a lid over medium-high heat until it's hot but not smoking. Add the garlic and cook until it smells toasty and turns a deep golden brown, about 3 minutes. Lower the heat to medium, add the basil, tomatoes, and salt, and give it a stir. Cook until the tomatoes have released some of their juice, turn the heat to low, and cook at a gentle simmer until the tomatoes are soft, sweet, and slightly thickened, 15 to 20 minutes.

Blend the sauce until it's smooth. Cover and put it in the fridge to chill.

Construct the trifle: Feed the tomato sauce and green goddess into separate pastry bags (or jerry-rig two resealable plastic bags). Drain off any liquid from the crabmeat. Drizzle a few tablespoons of the lemon dressing over the crab (just enough to brighten the crab without overwhelming its flavor), sprinkle the chives over it, and give it all a gentle toss. Grab 6 to 8 small glass jars. Put a layer of crab in the bottom of each jar, then a layer of green goddess, and then tomato sauce. Keep layering, finishing with crab on top. Cover with plastic wrap and put the trifle in the fridge for 15 minutes, so it's nice and cold. Serve straightaway.

MUSSELS STUFFED WITH MORTADELLA

I was sitting at an outdoor table at a café in Vernazza, one of the five spectacular little beach towns that make up the Cinque Terre, a rugged stretch of coast in north-western Italy, when I first tried this dish. My wineglass was full. The mussels were steamy and smelled of basil and tomatoes. Even better, each one had a little secret inside, a stuffing of ground veal and mortadella—like an elegant surf and turf. I was so taken with them that I asked if I could watch the chef make them. At dawn the next morning, I was in his kitchen. He spoke no English. I spoke no Italian. I got to cleaning mussels (I wasn't just going to sit there), then watched him do each step. I like to think my version is pretty close to his. Because today, when I make this dish, simply sopping up the briny, winy sauce with charred bread transports me back to Vernazza.   **serves 4**

FOR THE STUFFED MUSSELS

10 ounces pork or veal shoulder, cut into 1-inch pieces

One 5-ounce chunk mortadella, cut into 1-inch pieces

½ cup fine bread crumbs (see Bread Crumbs, page 12)

1½ teaspoons Maldon or another flaky sea salt

About 3 dozen large Prince Edward Island mussels,
cleaned and prepped (see A Note on Mussels, page 105)

FOR THE SAUCE

Three 28-ounce cans peeled whole tomatoes, drained, trimmed,
and squished with your hands

¼ cup extra virgin olive oil, plus a few glugs for finishing

7 medium garlic cloves, thinly sliced

¾ cup dry white wine, such as Sauvignon Blanc

1 or 2 Dutch or other spicy long red chili, thinly sliced (including seeds)

Maldon or another flaky sea salt

A small handful of basil leaves, roughly chopped

Special Equipment
Meat grinder or meat grinder attachment of a stand mixer

Make the stuffing: Put the pork or veal, mortadella, bread crumbs, and salt into a medium bowl and mix together thoroughly. Cover the bowl with plastic wrap and pop it into the freezer until the top layer goes a bit crunchy, about 1 hour.

Using a meat grinder (or the grinder attachment of a stand mixer), grind the meat through a large die into a bowl. Cover the mixture with plastic wrap and pop it into the freezer again until the top layer goes a bit crunchy, this time only 30 or so minutes.

Grind the mixture again through the small die.

Stuff the mussels: For each mussel, grab a generous tablespoon of the ground meat mixture, depending on the size of the mussels, and add it to one of the shell halves. Gently squeeze the shell until it's almost shut, then push any filling that oozes out back into the ground meat mixture. It's fine, though, if a bit of meat sticks to the outside of the shells—in fact, that'll help flavor the sauce. As you fill the mussels, place them in a big bowl. When you're done, you'll have a bowlful of almost-closed mussels, the pink filling peeking out through a crack in the black shells. (You might end up with a little extra stuffing, which you'll want to save and, perhaps, fry up the next day to eat with eggs.) Set the bowl of stuffed mussels aside while you start the sauce, or cover the bowl and refrigerate for up to a day.

Make the sauce: Reserve 3 cups of the squished tomatoes, and puree the rest in a food processor.

Pour the oil into an 8- to 9- quart Dutch oven or other pot large enough to hold the mussels in no more than two layers and turn the heat to medium-high. When the oil shimmers, add the garlic and cook, stirring constantly, until it turns a deep golden-brown color and smells nutty and sweet, about 2 minutes.

Add the wine, then add the squished tomatoes, tomato puree, chili, the reserved mussel liquor, 1 cup of water, and 1 teaspoon salt. Let the liquid come to a simmer and tweak the heat to maintain a gentle simmer for 5 minutes, stirring occasionally.

Cook the mussels: Add the mussels to the pot in one or two tightly packed layers. Don't just toss them in willy-nilly—if you do, the filling will fall out when you scoop them out later. Give them a gentle press down with your hands or a spoon.

Give the pot a gentle shake and cover the pot, tweaking the heat to maintain a gentle simmer.

Cook for about 25 minutes, then uncover the pot and give it a light shake. Spoon some of the liquid over the top of the mussels and replace the lid. Cook for 15 minutes more, shaking occasionally, turn off the heat, and let the mussels sit, lid still on, for 5 to 10 minutes.

Remove a mussel and open it. You should be able to easily pluck out the mussel meat and filling in one piece. Taste the sauce and add a little salt, if you'd like. Gently stir in the basil and a generous drizzle of olive oil. Bring the pot to the table along with large, shallow bowls and the grilled rustic bread.

A NOTE ON MUSSELS

First off, you want to buy mussels that are still alive. Any open ones should close as you clean them. If you spot one that doesn't, tap it lightly on your work surface and see if it closes. Discard any that don't. You always want mussels that feel heavy for their size. Happy mussels fill their shells with plump meat. If they're light, they've been starving or they're dead. Either way, they won't have much to offer. Before you get to cooking, scrub the mussels under running water with a rough sponge or brush to remove any sand and grit, and pull off any beards.

Prep the mussels over something like a large tray or baking sheet that will catch the mussel liquor but won't restrict your movements. Steady a mussel on its edge so that the flatter edge faces up. With the other hand, starting at the midpoint of the flatter edge, carefully force a small sharp knife into the space between the shell halves and use a light sawing motion to cut all the way around the shell's round tip. Twist your knife firmly but gently (be careful not to break the shell) to jimmy open the mussel. Use your fingers to pull the shell open as much as you can without separating the shell halves. Some of the mussel meat should be clinging to each side of the open shell. Remove any beard you see inside. Repeat this process with the remaining mussels. Strain the mussel liquor through a fine-mesh sieve into a bowl, and set it aside.

STEWED OCTOPUS WITH BUTTER BEANS

This is one of those dishes that makes you nod your head a bit as you eat it. It's quite simple—just the thing for anyone who thought octopus was a chore to cook—but it's not subtle. There's so much going on: the lovably snappy-tender octopus; the hearty beans and potato; the acidic tomatoes infused with sweet, aromatic garlic and fennel. Each bite makes you want another, and it's all light enough that you'll end up having many.

serves 4 to 6

FOR THE BEANS

1 cup dried butter beans, rinsed, picked over,
soaked overnight in water, and drained

7 garlic cloves, peeled

1 tablespoon extra virgin olive oil

1 tablespoon Maldon or another flaky sea salt

FOR THE STEW

One 4-pound or two 2-pound octopus (fully thawed if frozen)

5 tablespoons extra virgin olive oil

1 pound tomatoes, blanched, peeled, and cored (see Tomatoes, page 10)

2 small red onions, cut into ½-inch-thick half-moons

6 garlic cloves, halved lengthwise

1 medium fennel bulb, fronds reserved, tough outer layer removed
and root end trimmed, very roughly chopped

Maldon or another flaky sea salt

1 large cinnamon stick

2 medium Yukon Gold potatoes (about ¾ pound), peeled, rinsed
(see Potatoes, page 10), and cut into sixths

Aioli (see recipe, page 296) or
Green Goddess (see recipe, page 288); optional
Bruschetta (see Toast and Bruschetta, page 12; optional)

Cook the beans: Put the beans, garlic, and olive oil in a medium pot and cover them with cold water. Bring the water to a simmer over medium-low heat (don't rush it). Adjust the heat so the beans cook at a bare simmer and cook just until they're creamy on the inside, about 45 minutes if you used relatively fresh dried beans; older beans can take as long as 3 hours to get creamy. Stir in the salt.

Reserve 1 cup of the bean liquid and drain the beans; discard the garlic. (You can cook the beans a day or so in advance and store them in the refrigerator in a container along with their cooking liquid.)

Cook the octopus: Preheat the oven to 450°F.

Find an ovenproof pot roomy enough to hold the octopus snugly but with a little space to spare, and heat it—empty—over medium-high heat for about 5 minutes. Put the octopus, heads up (and side by side if using two), in the pot and drizzle with 1 tablespoon of the olive oil. Cover the pot and stick it in the oven. Cook the octopus, without toying with it, just until it's tender enough that you can easily stick a butter knife through the thick part of one of the legs, 1 to 1½ hours. As it cooks, the octopus will release a few cups of liquid and it'll end up braising in its own juices. When the octopus is done, remove the pot from the oven and let the octopus cool to room temperature in its liquid.

Remove the octopus from the pot, and reserve 1½ cups of the liquid. If you'd like, gently pull off the skin from the head of the octopus and the top of the legs (the skin may be anywhere from a pink to purple or crimson color) or gently scrape it off with a knife. Leave the skin on the bottom of the legs, where it meets the suction pads. Twist off the head—it should come off easily—and poke your finger through the center of the leg portion to push out the hard dime-sized spherical beak; discard the beak. Pull the head into elegant pieces and separate the legs but keep them more or less whole to show off their spindly curl. Set the octopus aside in a big bowl.

Cook the stew: Set a sieve over a bowl and gently tear the tomatoes into quarters over it, letting the juice drip into the bowl. Discard the seeds caught by the sieve and reserve the juice. Trim off and discard any pale, tough bits from the tomato chunks.

Heat the remaining ¼ cup olive oil in a 5- or 6-quart pot over medium heat, then add the onions, garlic, fennel, and a generous pinch of salt and cook until they soften, get a little golden, and start to stick to the pot as you stir, about 10 minutes. Add the cinnamon and stir, then add the tomato chunks and cook until the vegetables take on an orangey-red color, about 4 minutes.

Add the potatoes, beans, and the reserved bean cooking liquid, tomato juice, and octopus liquid to the pot. Bring to a simmer, tweaking the heat if necessary to maintain the simmer, and cook until the potatoes are cooked through and slightly crumbly, 20 to 30 minutes.

Add the octopus pieces, cover, and cook, gently stirring, until the octopus is hot. Taste and season with salt, if you'd like. Roughly chop enough of the reserved fennel fronds to give you a small handful and sprinkle them on top. Add the aioli or green goddess, if using, to the stew in little dollops. Bring the pot to the table with bowls and the bruschetta.

SEAFOOD SALAD

Here's a nice chilled salad that never fails to impress guests, so long as you take care not to overcook the seafood. That way, you'll have plump mussels, tender squid and clams, and hearty lobster to have at. (You can cook it all the day before, if you'd like.) I like to leave a few mussels and clams in their shells, so you can have a good old dig around while you're eating your salad, but that's up to you. Saffron aioli makes a colorful and tasty condiment to dollop here and there.   **serves 4**

1 large fennel bulb with stalks and fronds

1 cup dry white wine, such as Sauvignon Blanc

¼ teaspoon fennel seeds

5 strips lemon zest, about 3 inches long and ½ inch wide,
any white pith removed

1 medium shallot, thinly sliced

5 medium garlic cloves, roughly chopped

¾ pound mussels, scrubbed, debearded, and rinsed

1 pound Manila clams, scrubbed and rinsed

⅓ pound cleaned squid, bodies cut into ½-inch-wide rings

7 tablespoons extra virgin olive oil

One 1- to 1½-pound live lobster (see A Note on Lobster, page 113)

Maldon or another flaky sea salt

2 to 5 dried pequin chilies, crumbled, or pinches of red pepper flakes

1 tablespoon freshly squeezed lemon juice

About ¼ cup Saffron Aioli (see Note, page 296)

Cook the seafood: Remove the fronds from the fennel, wrap them in a damp paper towel, and reserve them in the fridge. Cut off the stalks and discard. Remove the outer layer of the fennel bulb and roughly chop it. Reserve the remaining bulb.

Pour the wine and 2 cups water into a medium pot with a lid and add the chopped fennel, fennel seeds, lemon zest, shallot, and half of the garlic. Set the pot over medium-high heat, cover it, and bring the liquid to a good simmer. Let the vegetables simmer for about 3 minutes, then remove the pot from the heat and let the aromatics steep in the covered pot for about 30 minutes.

Remove the lid and return the pot to high heat. As soon as the liquid comes to a rolling boil, add the mussels and cover the pot. Cook them, shaking the pot gently once or twice, just until they pop open, 1 to 2 minutes. (Sometimes bivalves behave themselves and open all at once, but sometimes they don't. So I like to peek into the pot now and then and remove them as they open.) As they open, scoop the mussels into a large bowl, doing your best to leave behind the liquid and aromatics. Discard any that haven't opened after 5 minutes.

Add the clams to the pot and repeat the process, transferring them to the bowl with the mussels. Strain the cooking liquid through a sieve into a medium bowl, discard the solids, and return the liquid to the pot.

Turn the heat to high again and let the liquid come back to a simmer. Add the squid to the pot and cover it. Cook, stirring once, just until the squid is opaque, about 1 minute. Add the squid to the bowl with the mussels and clams, let them cool, then cover the bowl with plastic wrap and pop it into the fridge to chill.

Reserve the liquid. There should be about 2 cups.

Trim off the root end of the fennel bulb and roughly chop the fennel into bite-sized pieces. Wipe out the pot or grab a large deep pan with a lid. Pour in 5 tablespoons of the olive oil and set the pot over medium-high heat. When the oil begins to smoke, add the lobster claws and wait 15 seconds or so, then add the other lobster pieces, flesh side down. After about 2 minutes, add the remaining chopped garlic and half of the chopped fennel.

Sprinkle in 1 teaspoon salt, crushing it between your fingers. Give the pot a shake and toss the contents, then cover the pot. Cook, stirring the vegetables occasionally and turning the lobster pieces once, just until the lobster shells turn red and the visible flesh turns white, about 8 minutes. Use tongs to transfer the lobster to a plate. Let it cool, cover it with plastic wrap, and pop it into the fridge to chill.

Making the dressing: Keep cooking the fennel and garlic, stirring frequently, for another 2 minutes. Add the reserved tomalley and cook, stirring frequently, until the vegetables begin to stick to the pot, about 1 minute more. Add the reserved shellfish cooking liquid, along with another teaspoon of salt and the chilies, and scrape the bottom as you stir to get at all those tasty bits. Bring the liquid to a vigorous simmer and simmer until it's reduced by half, 8 to 12 minutes. Remove the pot from the heat and let the mixture cool to room temperature. Then cover and refrigerate until chilled.

Assemble the salad: Toss the vegetable-tomalley mixture and all of the seafood together in a big bowl. Roughly chop the fennel fronds and add a five-fingered pinch to the bowl. Put the remaining chopped fennel bulb in a separate bowl and toss it with the lemon juice, the remaining 2 tablespoons olive oil, and a pinch of salt.

Arrange the seafood on a serving platter. Spoon the liquid left in the bottom of the bowl over the seafood, and scatter the dressed fennel on top. Dollop the aioli here and there, and serve straightaway.

A NOTE ON LOBSTER

If you're not up for killing a lobster yourself, you can ask your fishmonger to chop one into pieces, or leave it out altogether, letting extra mussels, clams, and squid fill its shoes. If you are up for it, put your live lobster on the cutting board and insert a heavy knife just behind the head (try not to be alarmed as it twitches). Bring the knife down with a firm motion, forcing it through the head to split it lengthwise. Halve the lobster lengthwise and chop it, shell on, into whatever size pieces you'd like to eat. Scoop out and save the dark-colored eggs, if you have a female lobster, for another purpose. Discard the stomach (the thin, grayish tube against the tail shell). Reserve the tomalley (which looks like a brain but is more like a liver) for this recipe. Let the lobster pieces drain for a minute or two on paper towels.

GRILLED SEA BASS

I could probably take down this whole fish by myself, crispy skin and all. You don't need much more than a salad and some bread to make it into a meal, but I urge you to try it with buttery Tomatoes Stewed with White Wine and Saffron (see recipe, page 215) and Lentil Puree (see recipe, page 243). If you like, stuff the fish with a few thin lemon slices and fresh herbs.   **serves 2 to 4**

One 1½- to 2-pound whole sea bass,
such as branzino or striped bass, scaled and gutted
Extra virgin olive oil
1 to 1½ tablespoons Maldon or another flaky sea salt
1 lemon, halved (optional)

About 15 minutes before you're ready to cook the fish, remove it from the fridge to take the chill off. Prepare a charcoal grill to cook with medium-high heat or heat a large grill pan or griddle over medium-high heat for about 10 minutes. You want your cooking surface to have a chance to get good and hot (though you don't want to burn the bugger).

Pat the fish dry with paper towels, then rub just enough olive oil all over it—including the head and tail—so that the whole thing is lightly, glossily coated. Season generously outside and inside with salt, crushing the grains between your fingers as you go.

Lay the fish on the hot cooking surface and cook for 4 minutes without messing with the fish. Rotate the fish to get nice cross-hatched grill marks and cook for another 4 minutes, occasionally lifting up the edge and peeking under to be sure it's browning nicely. You'll also want to lift and tilt it with a spatula for about 30 seconds every so often so that the flesh on its back makes contact with the hot surface. After about 8 minutes, the bottom side should be golden brown and the skin a bit crispy. Gently flip the fish over and do the same for the other side. It'll take another 8 to 10 minutes.

Carefully transfer the fish to a platter and let it rest for about 2 minutes. Add a drizzle of olive oil and a squeeze of lemon, if you'd like, and eat it straightaway.

HOW TO TELL WHEN YOUR FISH IS COOKED

I know some people get a bit nervous about how to tell when fish is perfectly cooked. You'll get better at it every time you cook fish, as you develop your instincts. But until then, try this: When you've cooked it on the second side for about 8 minutes, grab a skewer, the probe of a meat thermometer, or anything thin. Gently insert it into the side of the fish near its back, where the flesh is thickest. If your poker runs into bone without meeting any resistance along the way, the fish is fully cooked. If there is resistance, the fish needs a bit more time.

birds

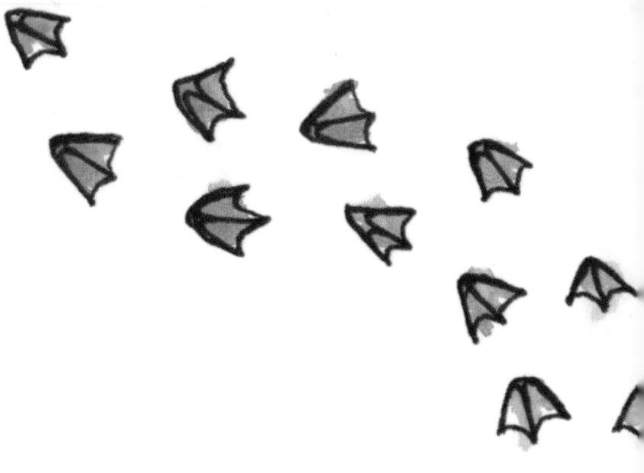

DUCK CONFIT

You can't have Cassoulet (see recipe, page 178) without duck confit, legs submerged in duck fat and cooked ever so slowly, but you should try making the confit even if you're not planning on burying it in beans. Duck confit makes a fine meal on its own once you brown the skin in a hot pan with some of the fat left over from simmering. You might serve it with a plate of lentils, beans, or potatoes, or pulled into shreds, the meat and crispy skin topping a salad of hearty greens.   **makes 2 confit duck legs**

12 black peppercorns

12 juniper berries

4 dried pequin chilies or pinches of red pepper flakes

½ small cinnamon stick

1 small thyme sprig, leaves only

4 medium garlic cloves, peeled

¼ cup kosher salt

2 duck legs (about ¾ pound each) with plenty of fatty skin

3 cups or so rendered duck fat

Mix together the peppercorns, juniper, chilies, and cinnamon in a mortar and crush them with the pestle until you have a mixture of fine and coarse bits. Add the thyme and garlic and crush again with the pestle. Put the salt in a small bowl and stir in the crushed mixture until well mixed.

Put the duck legs on a plate and sprinkle the salt mixture evenly all over them. Pat lightly so the mixture adheres. Cover the legs with plastic wrap and put them in the fridge overnight.

Warm the duck fat over very low heat in a small pot that will comfortably hold the duck legs until completely liquid. Rinse the spice mixture off the duck legs under running water and pat dry. Submerge the legs in the fat (if they're not submerged, switch to a different pot), tweak the heat if necessary to maintain a bare simmer (you should see only a bubble here and there), and cook until the meat comes away from the bone easily with the twist of a fork, about 2½ hours; stop before the meat begins to fall off the bone. Take the pot off the heat and let the duck cool in the fat. It will carry on cooking as it does.

Submerged in this lovely fat, the duck confit will keep, in a container covered with plastic wrap or a lid, in the fridge for several weeks.

ROAST CHICKEN WITH TOMATO-AND-BREAD SALAD

I do occasionally like a more elaborate roast chicken—perhaps some basil butter tucked underneath the skin—but here it's better simple, because you're serving it with a lovely salad.

A really nice panzanella, which is what this salad is, is all about getting the bread soggy and crispy at once. That makes it really nice to eat. To achieve this elusive texture, you must use stale bread and then toast it. That way, the croutons will be able to absorb some of the dressing without going all mushy. This is a classic panzanella, fantastic for showcasing summer tomatoes, preferably in an assortment of colors and sizes, whether you decide to follow my instructions and blanch and peel them (I like the ragged look and fleshy texture that gives them) or not.

serves 4

FOR THE BREAD SALAD

2¼ pounds firm but ripe summer tomatoes, blanched, peeled, and cored (see Tomatoes, page 10)

1 large garlic clove, peeled

Maldon or another flaky sea salt

4 whole salt-packed anchovies, rinsed, soaked, and filleted (see Filleting Salt-Packed Anchovies, page 10)

A very small handful of basil leaves, plus a few leaves for garnish

¼ cup extra virgin olive oil, plus a generous drizzle

2 tablespoons red wine vinegar

Freshly ground black pepper

Croutons (see Croutons, page 12), still slightly warm

FOR THE CHICKEN

One 4-pound chicken, patted dry

Kosher salt

2 tablespoons extra virgin olive oil

Marinate the tomatoes: Cut the tomatoes into very large chunks and trim off any hard or pale bits (if using cherry or grape tomatoes, leave them whole). Use your fingers to push out the seeds and juice from the tomato chunks into a small container, and reserve for another purpose. It's fine if you need to tear up the tomatoes a bit to get out the juices. Put the tomatoes in a large bowl.

Combine the garlic and a healthy pinch of salt in a mortar and pound it to a smooth paste. Add the anchovies and basil and pound again until you have a fairly smooth paste. (If you don't have a mortar, chop and mash the ingredients on a cutting board with a chef's knife.)

Combine the garlic-anchovy paste in a small bowl with the ¼ cup olive oil, the red wine vinegar, and a few twists of black pepper. Have a thorough stir, and pour the mixture over the tomatoes. Gently toss them around a bit so the dressing gets into every nook and cranny. Set them aside for at least 30 minutes. (You can refrigerate them, covered, for up to a day. Let them come to room temperature before you use them.)

Cook the chicken: Preheat the oven to 450°F. Let the chicken sit at room temperature for 15 minutes or so. Generously salt the chicken all over, including inside the cavity, and let it sit for another 15 minutes. Put the chicken in a roasting pan or baking dish, drizzle it with the olive oil, and pop it into the oven. Roast for 30 minutes, then reduce the heat to 400°F and continue to cook just until the skin is light golden brown and the juices run clear when you pierce the thickest part of the thigh, about 20 minutes more. Transfer the chicken to a cutting board and let it rest for 15 minutes.

Carve the chicken into pieces—drums, thighs, and breast slices.

Assemble the salad: Put the croutons in a bowl, drizzle half the tomato marinating liquid over them, and toss well. Arrange the bread and tomatoes on a platter so the rustic salad looks elegant, and drizzle on some or all of the remaining marinating liquid. Finish with a generous drizzle of olive oil and a sprinkling of basil leaves, and serve right away alongside the chicken.

MY CHICKEN ADOBO

I first had Filipino adobo years ago at a place in the East Village, and I fell in love straightaway, with the way the fat in the chicken rounded off the sharp edges of the vinegar, the way the flavors were so well married that no one of them stood out more than another. It was a dish at one with itself. I think mine's pretty close to that version. The soupy sauce is very aromatic and well balanced between the acidity of the vinegar, the saltiness of the soy sauce, and the sweetness of the onion, garlic, and ginger. I keep it really rustic—bone-in pieces of chicken, skin-on ginger, and peel-on garlic. Serve it with jasmine rice. **serves 6**

¼ cup peanut or canola oil

5 pounds bone-in, skin-on chicken legs and thighs,
hacked into approximately 2-inch pieces through
the bone by you or your butcher

2 heads garlic, cloves separated but not peeled

½ large Spanish onion, peeled and cut into 8 wedges

½ cup thinly sliced skin-on ginger

10 black peppercorns

4 fresh bay leaves, or 2 dried

1½ cups unseasoned rice vinegar

½ cup soy sauce

Heat the oil in a large pot that has a lid over high heat until it starts to smoke. Work in batches so you don't crowd the pot: Add half the chicken skin side down to the smoking oil and cook, turning the pieces over occasionally, until golden brown all over, 10 to 15 minutes. Transfer them to a plate and repeat with the second batch of chicken.

Add the garlic, onion, ginger, peppercorns, and bay leaves to the pot. Cook, stirring every now and again, until the onion goes translucent, about 10 minutes. You'll start to see lovely sticky, brown bits on the bottom of the pot. Add the chicken, then the vinegar and soy. Raise the heat to bring the liquid to a boil, scraping the pot to release the sweet, golden-brown bits stuck to it; the vinegar and soy will smell warm and inviting.

Cover the pot, lower the heat to maintain a gentle simmer, and cook, stirring occasionally, until the chicken is so tender you can easily pull it from the bone with a spoon, about 45 minutes. Serve in large bowls.

GUINEA FOWL SALAD WITH
FIGS AND CIPOLLINI ONIONS

This salad has layers of textures and flavors: fleshy marinated figs; creamy, sweet cipollini onions; and salty, juicy pieces of guinea fowl, a full-flavored game bird that you can order at nearly any good butcher shop. A few handfuls of whatever sprightly greens you find at the market lighten it up, though alongside crusty bread, I'd serve the salad as a lovely meal for two.

serves 2 to 4

⅓ cup plus 2 teaspoons extra virgin olive oil

½ teaspoon nice, thick balsamic vinegar

1 teaspoon packed finely grated lemon zest

2 teaspoons freshly squeezed lemon juice

⅛ teaspoon very finely chopped garlic

1½ teaspoons thyme leaves, preferably lemon thyme, chopped

Kosher salt

5 ripe medium Mission figs, stems trimmed, halved lengthwise

About ½ pound small cipollini onions, all roughly the same size, peeled

One 2½- to 3½-pound guinea hen (see Note)

3 handfuls mixed market greens (perhaps wild arugula,
pea shoots, dandelion, and sunflower sprouts)

A 1-ounce chunk of Parmesan

Stir together 2 teaspoons of the olive oil, the balsamic, lemon zest and juice, garlic, thyme, and a generous pinch of salt in a large mixing bowl. Add the figs and toss to coat them well. Let the figs marinate for 1 hour at room temperature.

Meanwhile, heat the remaining ⅓ cup of olive oil in a small pan over medium-low heat until it shimmers. Add the onions, along with a generous pinch of salt, and cook, turning them over every now and then, until they're light golden brown and very soft, about 20 minutes. Take the pan off the heat and let the onions cool in the oil. Season with salt.

While the onions are cooling, heat a cast-iron griddle or grill pan over medium heat until very hot, about 5 minutes. Put the guinea hen pieces skin side up on a plate and season generously with salt. If the breast meat is much thicker than the thigh meat, separate them before cooking. Put the hen skin side down on the griddle and lightly season the side facing up with salt. Cook until the skin is golden brown and crispy, 8 to 10 minutes, then flip and cook until the meat is just cooked through at the thickest part, 3 to 5 minutes more. Transfer it to a plate to rest for a few minutes.

Cut the guinea hen into pieces and arrange half of them on a platter. Remove the onions from the oil. Put the onions and half the figs here and there on the platter. Gently toss the greens in the dressing left in the bowl of figs, and scatter about half the greens over the hen and figs. Arrange the remaining guinea hen, figs, and greens on top in layers, seasoning each layer with salt. Shave on the Parmesan, spoon on a few spoonfuls of the cipollini cooking oil, if you'd like, and serve.

Note: Preorder a guinea hen from a butcher shop. Ask the butcher to halve and separate the bird length-wise and debone each half, leaving the leg meat attached to the breast meat and the drumette attached to the breast, but the wing snipped off. Feel free to substitute deboned pigeon, quail, or even chicken, if you must.

cow

BEEF AND BAYLEY HAZEN PIE

I love hauling this pie to the table and seeing the looks on people's faces. The slightly sweet, deep-golden crust, both flaky and crunchy, is pretty enough, but then you crack into it and out tumbles an avalanche of steamy beef and blue cheese. It's a grander version of the handheld meat pies I ate growing up. I always fancied the ones filled with beef and Stilton, which complement each other quite well, but since I've been in the U.S., I've fallen for the funk of Bayley Hazen, a fantastic blue cheese made by Jasper Hill Creamery in Vermont. Pints of stout and a salad of bitter greens are all you need alongside. **serves 6 to 8**

FOR THE BEEF FILLING

2 pounds boneless short ribs,
cut into approximately 1- by 2-inch pieces

1 tablespoon kosher salt

¼ cup all-purpose flour

About ½ cup extra virgin olive oil

2 heads garlic, cloves separated and peeled

2 medium Spanish onions, halved lengthwise and thickly sliced

2 tablespoons thyme leaves, chopped

1½ tablespoons black peppercorns, coarsely crushed

3 cups dry red wine

3 cups Sticky Chicken Stock (see recipe, page 302)

FOR THE SUET DOUGH

3 cups all-purpose flour, plus extra for dusting

1 tablespoon baking powder

2 teaspoons kosher salt

1½ cups (about ⅓ pound) freshly ground suet, chilled

About ¼ cup ice-cold water

FOR FINISHING THE PIE

Room-temperature butter for the pan

About ⅓ pound Bayley Hazen Blue or Stilton

Note:
This recipe might look a bit elaborate, but you make the beef for the filling and the pastry the day before you plan to serve it.

1 egg yolk

1 tablespoon whole milk

Special Equipment
A nonstick springform pan, 8 inches in diameter
and 3 inches deep; a pastry brush

Make the filling: Put the meat into a big bowl and season it evenly all over with the salt. Add the flour and toss to evenly coat every piece.

Put a wide, heavy ovenproof pot over high heat and pour in half of the olive oil. When it begins to smoke, brown the meat on all sides, in batches with the remaining olive oil, if necessary, about 10 minutes per batch. Transfer the meat to a plate. Add the garlic, onions, thyme, and pepper to the pot, and cook, without stirring, for about 3 minutes. Return the meat to the pot, stir well, and cook for 10 minutes, stirring now and again. The bottom of the pot should be deep brown and the onions slightly soft. Pour in the red wine, stir, and bring to a simmer. Turn the heat down to maintain a gentle simmer, and cook until the liquid looks a little viscous, about 15 minutes.

Add the stock, let it return to a simmer, cover the pot, and cook at a gentle simmer until the meat is tender enough to come apart easily between your fingers, about 2 hours. Let the filling cool in the pot, cover it with a lid, and chill overnight in the fridge.

Make the dough: Mix together the flours, baking powder, and salt in a medium bowl, then mix in the suet. Add ¼ cup of the water, stirring the mixture with a fork and gradually adding more water if you need it, until you have a slightly sticky dough with the fat well distributed rather than in large chunks. Cover with plastic wrap and chill for at least 2 hours and up to 24 hours.

The next day, finish and bake the pie: Remove the meat from the pot and put it in a large bowl. You'll have about 5 cups of solidified liquid remaining in the pot. Put the pot over medium-high heat, bring the liquid to a boil, and cook, stirring often to make sure the onion doesn't stick to the bottom, until it reduces by half, about 45 minutes.

Meanwhile, break the chunks of meat into smaller pieces. Let the reduced liquid cool completely and pour over the meat. Give it a gentle stir. (To cool it quickly, set the bowl in another slightly larger bowl filled with ice water and stir often.)

Coat the sides and bottom of the springform pan with a light layer of butter.

Make a rough ball from about three-quarters of the dough, keeping the rest in the fridge. Dust your work surface with flour and roll out the dough ball into a 14-inch disk. Place it in the pan, gently pressing it against the bottom and up the sides so it fits securely. Chill the pie shell in the fridge for at least 15 minutes (it can be refrigerated for as long as overnight).

Preheat the oven to 350°F. Spoon half of the beef filling into the chilled pie shell. Crumble half of the cheese into large hunks (not little crumbly bits) and scatter over the filling. Spoon in the remaining filling and scatter on the rest of the cheese in the same large hunks.

Dust the work surface with flour again. Form a rough ball with the remaining dough and roll it into a 10-inch round. Use a 1-inch round pastry cutter or a small knife to cut a circle in the center of this round; remove the little circle of dough and set it aside for the moment.

Whisk together the egg yolk and milk in a small bowl. Use a pastry brush to brush the rim of the pie with some of the egg mixture. Lay the 10-inch round on top of the pie and press it lightly against the rim of the bottom crust until it adheres. Trim off any overhang with a knife, reserve it, and crimp the edges of the pie.

Form the reserved dough scraps into a ball. Lightly flour your surface once more and roll out the dough into a disk about ¼ inch thick. Use a 2-inch pastry cutter or a knife to cut out a circle from the dough, then use a 1-inch cutter or a knife to cut out the center. You'll have an O-shaped piece of dough.

Brush the top of the pie with the egg mixture, and place the O of dough on top so the holes line up. (Reserve the remaining egg mixture.) Chill for about 15 minutes. Brush the top of the pie again with the egg mixture and bake, rotating the pan occasionally, until the crust is crispy and golden brown all over, about 1½ hours.

Put the pan on a rack and use a knife to make sure the sides of the crust have separated from the pan. Let it rest for 25 minutes. Carefully loosen the spring and remove the ring. Cut into wedges and serve.

SKIRT STEAK WITH WATERCRESS AND CHILIES

This is my not-so-Thai salad, inspired by those bright heaps of meat and herbs—but quite different. Peppery watercress stands in for the typical mint and cilantro used in Thai salads. Tomatoes provide texture and pops of acidity, and I love how the shallots absorb some of the lime dressing and go a bit pickly. Add tender skirt steak, which just beats the pants off the more sought-after hanger cut, and it's perfect—well, almost. To me, the heat and flavor of the scorched chilies are what takes the salad from just pleasing to thrilling.   **serves 4**

1 packed teaspoon finely grated lime zest

2 tablespoons freshly squeezed lime juice

¼ cup extra virgin olive oil, plus a few glugs

1½ teaspoons Dijon mustard

⅛ teaspoon finely grated garlic

½ teaspoon Maldon or another flaky sea salt

A 1-pound skirt steak, cut in half or thirds, if necessary

Kosher salt

2 large Dutch or other spicy long red chilies,
thinly sliced (including seeds)

3 medium shallots, root ends trimmed, halved lengthwise,
and cut lengthwise into thin slices

1 pint or so cherry tomatoes, halved

2 big fistfuls (about 3 ounces) peppery baby watercress

Preheat a grill to high (preferably, build a charcoal fire and let the coals turn pale gray) or heat a cast-iron griddle over high heat. Let the grates or griddle get good and hot.

Whisk together the lime zest, juice, extra virgin olive oil, mustard, garlic, and sea salt in a small bowl. Set the dressing aside for the moment.

Rub both sides of the steak with a generous drizzle of oil, then generously season all over with the kosher salt. Scatter one side with half the chilies and give them a good old pat so they stick, then flip the steak and do the same on the other side. Grill the steak, turning it over once, until it's charred and lovely looking, 4 to 6 minutes for medium-rare. Some of the chilies will fall onto the hot surface. Pluck

Note:

I pat the sliced chilies onto the steak so they stick, then char the steak over really high heat. But in a kitchen without good ventilation, you might end up overtaken by chili smoke. So, before you get going, open a window and turn on the fan, or grill outside, with a griddle to keep the chilies from falling in between the grates.

them off with tongs as they get charred and put them in a large bowl. When the steak is ready, add it to the bowl, folding it if need be.

Spoon about 2 teaspoons of the dressing over the steak and chilies and give it a toss.

Combine the shallots and tomatoes in a large bowl, pour in the rest of the dressing, and give it a toss. Let it sit for a couple of minutes, then add the watercress and toss gently but well.

Slice the steak across the grain into long, thin slices, about 5 inches long and a little less than ¼ inch thick. Layer the salad and steak, lightly and elegantly, on a platter, ending with a small handful of the vegetables. Spoon on the lovely liquid remaining in the steak bowl and scatter any remaining chilies here and there.

GRILLED RIB EYE WITH ROMESCO

The rib eye is hands down the tastiest part of the cow, especially when it's thick and cooked to a juicy medium-rare. It's fun to cook too, to watch it develop a crust that's all sweet and salty with little crunchy bits that inspire you to take another and yet another bite. The bright romesco sauce—a little smoky, sweet, and tart—served alongside provides relief from the richness and elevates the steaks to another level. Serving Chimichurri (see recipe, page 292) or Salsa Verde (see recipe, page 289) would be quite nice as well.   **serves 4**

Two 2½-inch-thick bone-in rib-eye steaks (about 2 pounds each)
Kosher salt
½ lemon
A few glugs of extra virgin olive oil
10 small spring onions or scallions, roots trimmed, dry outer layer removed
Romesco Sauce (see recipe, page 293)

Light a charcoal fire, let the flames die down, and wait until the coals ash over, then push the coals to one side of the grill. Alternatively, use a gas grill or preheat a grill pan over medium heat.

Generously season the steaks all over with salt. Let them stand at room temperature for 10 minutes. This will help the steaks cook evenly.

Put the steaks on the grill over the area with no coals or directly in the hot area of the gas grill or grill pan, and cook, uncovered, until the bottom has a lovely dark-brown crust, about 15 minutes; rotate the steaks after about 7 minutes to get nice cross-hatched grill marks. Use tongs to gently flip the steaks and cook the second side the same way you did the first. Transfer the steaks to a cutting board, squeeze on a little lemon juice, and drizzle on plenty of olive oil. Let them rest for about 8 minutes.

While the steaks are resting, grill the spring onions or scallions, flipping them once, until they're a bit charred and the bulbs give slightly when you squeeze them, 5 to 8 minutes. Season to taste with salt and olive oil.

Use a sharp knife to cut the steaks across the grain into ½-inch-thick slices. (Don't forget to season the bone, as there's always someone at the table who will want to nibble on it.) Serve the steak and spring onions on a platter, juices, bones, and all. Spoon some romesco sauce onto the slices or serve it in a bowl alongside.

Note:
Find yourself a good butcher who sells thick rib-eye steaks that are stippled with white fat. Even better, have him cut 2½-inch-thick steaks to order from the rib section. A really thick steak is essential, because if it's too thin, it won't develop as lovely a crust.

TONGUE SANDWICHES

I learned to make *bollito misto*, a remarkably simple but delicious Italian dish of boiled meats, from Rose and Ruth at The River Café in London. My favorite bit was the tongue, with its powerfully beefy flavor and luscious tenderness after hours of cooking. Equally inspiring were the condiments the *bollito misto* came with: nose-tingling horseradish and bright, salty *dragoncello*, a sauce made from tarragon, eggs, anchovies, and mustard. When I was working on the menu for The Breslin, I had a "wouldn't-that-be-nice-on-bread" moment, something that happens to me quite a bit. So I reimagined The River Café's *bollito misto* as a sandwich, soft slices of tongue on a crusty baguette, set off by a spark of condiments. Unless you like overstuffed sandwiches, you'll definitely have tongue left over. It keeps in the fridge for 2 days and in the freezer for a month.

makes 4 sandwiches

FOR THE TONGUE

1 beef tongue (about 3 pounds),
trimmed of any firm or hard bits

Simple Brine (see recipe, page 143)

1 medium carrot, peeled

2 medium celery stalks

1 head garlic, halved horizontally

½ medium Spanish onion

1 fresh bay leaf, or ½ dried

FOR THE SANDWICHES

1 long, wide baguette

Extra virgin olive oil

Maldon or another flaky sea salt (optional)

About ⅓ cup Tarragon Sauce (see recipe, page 290)

About ¼ cup finely grated peeled fresh horseradish

A few handfuls of arugula

Make the tongue: Put the tongue in a very large bowl or medium pot (you might have to bend it to get it to fit), cover it with the brine, and put it in the fridge, covered, for 5 days, turning it once.

Drain the tongue and rinse it well under cold running water. At this point, you can wrap the tongue in plastic and refrigerate it until you're ready to cook it, up to 2 days.

Put the tongue in a large pot, cover it with water, and bring to a boil over high heat, then immediately drain the tongue. (This will help get rid of some of the scum.) Put the tongue back in the pot and add the carrot, celery, garlic, onion, and bay leaf, along with enough water to cover it by an inch or so. Bring the water to a boil, turn the heat down so it simmers gently, cover the pot, and cook at a gentle simmer just until you can stick a sharp knife into the tongue without any resistance, 4 to 5 hours. The tongue should still hold its shape; you don't want it so tender that it's falling apart. Remove the pot from the heat, gently remove the tongue (don't dump the liquid), put it on a plate or cutting board, and let it sit until it's just cool enough to handle.

Gently peel off the thin outer layer of the tongue, which is really fun and satisfying to do. It should come off with ease. Discard it, trim off any gristly bits, return the tongue to the cooking liquid, and set it aside to cool until it reaches room temperature.

Remove the tongue from the liquid and pat it dry with paper towels. Wrap it in plastic and pop it into the fridge to firm up, at least an hour or up to 2 days.

When you're ready to make the sandwiches, slice the cold tongue crosswise into enough ½-inch-thick slices to fill the sandwiches with one layer.

Make the sandwiches: Cut the baguette into 4 equal pieces and split each one lengthwise in half, stopping just before you reach the other side, creating a sort of bun. Put a grill, griddle, or cast-iron skillet over medium heat until it's nice and hot. Toast the baguette buns (first the bottom, then the top) on the hot surface just until the outsides are crispy but the middles are still soft.

Use the same grill for the tongue. Have a nibble of tongue to see if you'd like to add a little salt before you grill it. Lightly rub each slice of tongue with olive oil, sprinkle on a little salt if you'd like, and add the slices to the grill. (Grill in batches if you need to in order to avoid crowding.) Cook the slices until they're nice and brown on both sides, flipping once, 4 to 6 minutes total.

Open the baguette pieces and spread the tarragon sauce evenly on both sides. Add a layer of tongue to each piece of baguette, and top it off with a little grated horseradish and some arugula. Close the sandwiches, give them a gentle squish with your palm, and serve.

SIMPLE BRINE

A dip in this simple brine will infuse meat with flavor and keep it from drying out as it cooks. I use it for Tongue Sandwiches (see recipe, page 141), but you can use it in simpler dishes too, like roast chicken or pork, as long as you cut back dramatically on the peppercorns and cloves.   **makes 3 quarts**

1 cup kosher salt
2 tablespoons black peppercorns
1 tablespoon whole cloves
3 fresh bay leaves, or 2 dried
¾ teaspoon No. 1 curing salt (optional; see Note)

Combine the salt, peppercorns, cloves, and bay leaves with 4 cups water in a large pot. Bring the water to a boil, stirring to help dissolve the salt.

Remove the pot from the heat, add 8 cups cold water, and give it a good stir. Cover and put it in the fridge until it's cold before using. The brine keeps in the fridge for up to 5 days.

Note:
In order for the brine to penetrate the dense muscle, you have to brine the tongue for 5 days before cooking. To ensure the cooked tongue has a nice color, I like to stir ¾ teaspoon curing salt into the cold brine before adding the tongue.

STUFFED VEAL BREAST

Here's yet another dish whose success relies on a balancing act: butterflied veal breast, tender with a little chewiness to it, wrapped around a stuffing made of ground veal, prosciutto, and mozzarella, among other tasty things. The bright sauce, made with white wine and tomato, and stuffing have a lot of flavor—those capers and pro-sciutto add up to a lot of umami. Yet you can still taste the veal, delicate and rich at once, as well as sweet in that subtle way meat can be sweet. It's an exciting dish to haul out for friends or family. It also reheats well, whether whole or in slices. Any leftovers make a fine sandwich. **serves 8**

FOR THE STUFFING

Veal chunks reserved from butterflying the breast (see Note)

½ pound prosciutto, cut into 1-inch pieces
(ask for the cheaper "end" or "hock meat")

½ pound fresh, creamy mozzarella,
preferably mozzarella di bufalo, drained and torn into chunks

½ cup pine nuts, toasted in a dry pan over medium heat until golden

About 4 cups lightly packed chunks day-old
rustic bread with crusts removed

3 large garlic cloves, very finely chopped

A large handful of flat-leaf parsley leaves

2 tablespoons extra virgin olive oil

8 dried pequin chilies or pinches of red pepper flakes

1 tablespoon Maldon or another flaky sea salt

One 6-pound boned veal breast, butterflied (see Note)

Kosher salt

FOR THE SAUCE

½ cup extra virgin olive oil

Maldon or another flaky sea salt

8 medium garlic cloves, thinly sliced

A small handful of basil leaves, roughly chopped

5 dried pequin chilies, crumbled, or pinches of red pepper flakes

2 cups drained, trimmed, and chopped
canned peeled whole tomatoes

1½ cups dry white wine, such as Sauvignon Blanc, plus a few glugs
3 tablespoons drained capers, chopped

Special Equipment
A meat grinder or grinder attachment of a stand mixer;
butcher's twine

Stuff the breast: Put the veal chunks in a medium bowl, cover the bowl with plastic wrap, and pop it into the freezer until the edges get crunchy, about 1 hour. Chill the mozzarella and prosciutto in the fridge, if necessary. Combine the veal chunks, pine nuts, bread, prosciutto, mozzarella, garlic, and parsley in a large mixing bowl. Toss well with your hands, giving it all a good squish. Drizzle in the olive oil, crumble in the chilies, and sprinkle in the salt, crushing it between your fingers. Give it all another good toss.

Grind the mixture through the medium die of a meat grinder into a bowl. Squish and mix it just until everything is well distributed.

Lay the breast fat side down. Lightly season the side of the veal breast facing up with salt. Spread the stuffing mixture over the breast in an even layer, leaving a ½-inch border around three edges and a 1½-inch border on the longer edge, near the fatty part. Starting from a long edge, roll up the meat so you have a fairly tight cylinder. Turn it seam side down and use butcher's twine to tie it crosswise in about seven places. (You can do this up to a day ahead; cover with plastic wrap and keep in the fridge.)

Preheat the oven to 300°F.

Sear the breast and make the sauce: Add the olive oil to a flameproof baking dish or roasting pan large enough to hold the stuffed breast and heat it over medium-high heat until it smokes. Season the stuffed breast with salt and put it in the hot oil, fat side down. Cook, turning the breast and rotating the pan occasionally, until it's golden brown all over, 10 to 15 minutes.

Transfer the breast to a platter. Return any stuffing that falls to the pan; it'll help flavor the sauce. Turn the heat to low, add the garlic, and cook, stirring frequently, until it's toasty and light golden brown, about 4 minutes. Add half the basil and the chilies and cook, stirring and scraping the bottom of the pan, for about 3 minutes, then stir in the tomatoes, white wine, and capers. Bring it to a gentle simmer.

Return the breast to the pan and pop it into the oven. Cook for about 4½ hours, basting the breast occasionally and piling some of the tomatoes on top, until you can easily stick a fork into the meat. If the liquid in the pan starts looking thick, pour in a cup of water, or a few more glugs of white wine if you'd like to add more acidity.

Remove the veal breast from the oven and set it on a cutting board. Let it rest for 30 minutes. Untie the veal, cut it into eight 1- to 1½-inch-thick slices, and serve the slices on plates with plenty of the sauce and the remaining basil.

Note: Veal breast comes with the bone in, and it can be larger or small, depending on how the butcher cuts it. For this recipe, tell your butcher you want a veal breast with the bones removed. You want to end up with a big old rectangular breast that's about 15 inches long, 9 inches wide, and about 2 inches thick.

To prep it for this recipe, find the narrow end of the breast (at the neck end) and trim off an approximately 9-by-3-inch (1-pound) piece from that end. Cut this piece into 1-inch chunks and set them aside.

You can also ask the butcher to butterfly the breast, but that part is easy enough for even a novice. Turn the veal breast so one of the shorter sides is facing you. Now you're going to butterfly the breast, cutting it so it opens like a book: Use a very sharp knife held parallel to the cutting board to make short, sure incisions starting in the middle of one of the long sides. Every few cuts you make will let you open the breast a little bit more. Stop just before you reach the other side, and open the breast out flat. If you end up with any holes in the meat, find a portion of breast that's slightly thicker than the rest, shave off a small piece from it with your knife, and use it to patch the holes.

dinner with marcella

A while back, I was feeling a bit down and out. So my mate Fergus Henderson and I went out for a drink. Sitting next to him, I nursed a glass of champagne, trying to boost my mood with bubbles. Then Fergus did it for me. "I know what you need," he said. "Come see Marcella with me."

I immediately felt lighter at the prospect. Marcella Hazan is a hero of mine—a deity, really. She did for Italian food in America what Julia Child did for French. Similar story, too. Hazan wasn't a chef or professional of any sort. She learned to cook to impress a man who eventually became her husband. At least, that's how the story goes.

Soon enough, I was on a plane not to Venice but to Sarasota, Florida, where Marcella lives.

The next day, Fergus and I were waiting, nervous and sweaty, for the elevator in her building, which seemed to take forever to come. When her husband, Victor, opened the door, I saw Marcella behind him, an elegant little gray-haired woman. We sat down at a coffee table where a bunch of little treats were set out. Even though I didn't see white truffles on the table, I could smell them. I remember thinking, for a second, How fitting, she smells like white truffles!

Marcella gestured at a bowl filled with orbs the size of olives and asked in her husky, heavily accented English if we knew what they were. We didn't. Baby peaches, she said, soaked in truffle oil. I laughed to myself—so it wasn't the way she smelled all the time.

Soon it was lunchtime and we gathered with the other guests around a bottle of Barolo at the table. Marcella had made green pappardelle with ragù—veal, mushrooms, and a bit of tomato, all in perfect balance. The noodles had crinkly edges and were irregularly shaped, some bigger than others. It was beautiful. She explained that hers always had visible specks of spinach so people knew it was homemade. I ate two bowlfuls.

She ate with us, then disappeared into the kitchen to finish preparing the next course. When she emerged, she was trailing a helper holding a platter. On it, two massive veal shanks, roasted with little more than garlic and white wine, stood bone up. That was exciting enough, but then she took two spoons and stuck them inside the hollow of the bone, into the marrow.

Fergus, whose name has sort of become synonymous with marrow, was distracted, talking to someone else at the table, and I saw my chance to make his day as he had made mine when he'd suggested the visit. I leaned over and told him what I'll tell you now: You're going to like what comes next.

ROASTED VEAL SHANKS
WITH WHITE WINE AND SHALLOTS

This is my attempt at re-creating Marcella's fantastic veal shanks (see Dinner with Marcella, page 148). Hers weren't falling-off-the-bone tender, which I really liked. Instead, she slowly roasted the meat to bring out its stickiness but stopped before it lost its lovely chewiness. The touch of sweetness from the melting shallots and acidity from a splash of white wine are the only embellishments the veal needs.

serves 4

1 veal fore shank (about 4½ pounds), without the knuckle,
bone cut to reveal the marrow

About ¼ cup extra virgin olive oil

About 1½ tablespoons Maldon
or another flaky sea salt

5 medium shallots, thinly sliced

3 medium skin-on garlic cloves

About ¾ cup dry white wine, such as Sauvignon Blanc

Salsa Verde (see recipe, page 289; optional)

Preheat the oven to 400°F.

Put the shank in a roasting pan or baking dish. Drizzle all over with the olive oil and rub the oil into the meat, then season it liberally with salt. Roast the shank for 2 hours, turning it over every now and then.

Lower the heat to 300°F and scatter the shallots and garlic around the shank. Cook, knocking the shallots and garlic around occasionally, until they look soft and light golden brown, about 10 minutes. Pour a splash of the white wine over and around the shank, and keep cooking, adding a splash of wine every 15 minutes or so and basting occasionally, until the shank is tender but has a slight, almost crunchy chewiness (the meat should not be falling off the bone), about 1½ hours more. If you run out of wine before the end of cooking, you can add a little splash of water, just to keep things moist.

Transfer the shank to a cutting board and let it rest for 10 minutes. Meanwhile, pour ¼ cup water into the roasting pan, set it over high heat, and bring to a boil as you stir and scrape the bottom with a wooden spoon to get at all the caramelized bits. Turn off the heat, add salt to taste, and set aside while you slice the shank.

Cut the meat perpendicular to the bone into ¼- to ½-inch-thick slices. Put them on a plate and top with the pan juices. Spoon the salsa verde, if using, here and there.

a girl and her pig

a little lamb

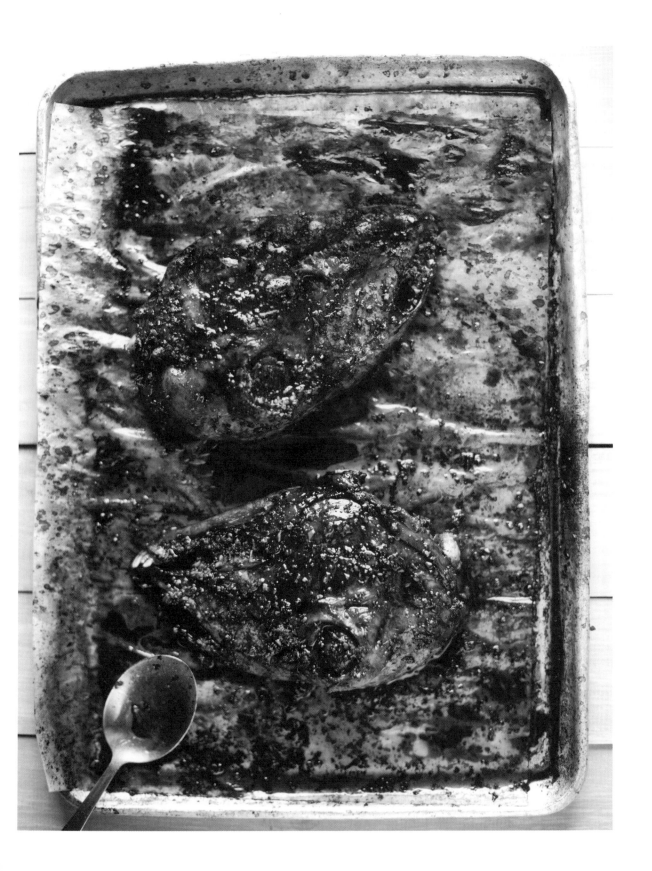

A LAMB'S HEAD

What a gorgeous thing—a lamb's head all deep brown from a slow cook in the oven, perfect for anyone who likes nibbling on bones. It's such a treat discovering all the different textures in the head: some bits creamy and sticky, others tender with a nice chew, the custardy brain, the meaty deposit behind the eye. Then there's my very favorite bit: the crispy stuff you get to peel from the jaw. I love swiping it through some of the wine that's become syrupy at the bottom of the pan. Once you've found a lamb's head—talk to your butcher or ask around at the farmers' market—the rest is simple. You stick it in the oven, drizzle on some red wine every so often, and more or less forget it's in there.   **serves 4**

1 brain-in, tongue-in lamb's head (3 to 4 pounds),
skinned and split lengthwise by your butcher
Kosher salt
About ¼ cup extra virgin olive oil
2 medium garlic cloves, smashed and peeled
2 tablespoons rosemary leaves
About 1½ cups Chianti or other robust red wine

Special Equipment
Parchment paper

Preheat the oven to 300°F. Line a rimmed baking sheet with parchment paper.

Generously season both halves of the head (cut sides too) with salt. Put the halves cut side down on the baking sheet, lightly drizzle olive oil all over the face, and pop the head into the oven.

Toss the garlic and rosemary together on a cutting board and chop very fine, until they're melded together. When you're done, the mixture will look a bit like blue cheese. Put the mixture in a small bowl, stir in 2 tablespoons of the olive oil, and let it sit while the head roasts.

After 1 hour, take a look at your head. It will have browned slightly, and you'll see more of the teeth showing. Spoon the garlic mixture evenly over the face and put it back in the oven.

Once the garlic has turned golden brown, about 30 minutes, pour a generous

Note:

Make sure the head is really fresh, because the brain and tongue don't keep well. If you have a choice, do as you would if you were shopping for fish and buy the head with the clearest, glassiest eyes.

¼ cup of the wine over the head halves to moisten them well. Cook for another 30 minutes, adding a similar splash of wine every 10 minutes. Drizzle a little more olive oil over each half, and add a similar splash of wine. Cook for another 10 minutes, basting the head three or four times so the flavors really mingle. The head should look dark, sticky, and beautiful, and the baking sheet should be almost completely covered with a sticky, winey residue.

Take the head out of the oven and give the cheek (the pocket of meat below the eye and next to the teeth) a poke with a knife. If it sinks right into the meat with barely any resistance, the head is ready. Larger heads will need a bit longer. Tip the baking sheet so the juices, oil, and wine collect in a corner. Give it a taste. It's good, isn't it?

Spoon some juices over each half, give the head another sprinkle of salt, and let it rest for 5 minutes or so. Serve on a platter or in the baking pan with glasses filled with any wine left in the bottle.

LAMB MEATBALLS WITH YOGURT, EGGS, AND MINT

These are *not* straight-up Italian meatballs. The sauce has a bit of North Africa as well as the Mediterranean in it, so the dish is exotic and comforting at once. The sauce has a whiff of cumin and mint, both good friends to ground lamb. Just before I serve the meatballs, I add little blobs of yogurt, crack a few eggs into the pot, and let them poach. **serves 4**

FOR THE MEATBALLS

2½ pounds boneless lamb shoulder, cut into 1-inch pieces

2½ tablespoons Maldon or another flaky sea salt

½ pound (about 2 cups) fine bread crumbs
(see Bread Crumbs, page 12)

1 tablespoon extra virgin olive oil

FOR THE SAUCE

1 large Spanish onion, finely chopped

5 garlic cloves, thinly sliced

½ teaspoon Maldon or another flaky sea salt

2 teaspoons coriander seeds, toasted and ground (see Spices, page 9)

1½ teaspoons cumin seeds, toasted and ground (see Spices, page 9)

2 Dutch or other spicy long red chilies, pierced with a sharp knife

One 28-ounce can peeled whole tomatoes, drained, trimmed,
and squished with your hands

About ½ cup whole-milk Greek-style yogurt

4 large eggs

FOR FINISHING

A small handful of mint leaves

A small handful of small, delicate cilantro sprigs

Extra virgin olive oil

Special Equipment
Meat grinder or meat grinder attachment of a stand mixer

For meatballs, you want to use light, airy, delicate ground meat, which is why I like to grind it myself. Often the ground meat you see on supermarket shelves is already overmixed, paste-like and sticky. You can use either a dedicated meat grinder or the attachment for your stand mixer. Before I form my meatballs, I like to roll a tester and fry it in a pan to check the seasoning (and because it makes a nice little snack).

Make the meatballs: Put the lamb in a large mixing bowl, cover the bowl with plastic wrap, and pop it into the freezer until the edges get crunchy, about 1 hour.

Toss the lamb well with the salt, then add the bread crumbs and toss again. Use a meat grinder (or the grinder attachment of a stand mixer) to grind the mixture through a medium die into a bowl. Put the mixture through the medium die once more.

Take a bit of the mixture in your hand, give it a few firm but still rather gentle squeezes, and roll it into a ball (you're shooting for each one to be a little bigger than a golf ball). Overworking the mixture is bad and leads to tough meatballs, but this warning often makes cooks too timid when they form the balls: the outside of each ball should be smooth, with no big cracks or crags. Gently pinch any cracks closed so the ball doesn't fall apart in the pan. Repeat with the remaining mixture.

Add the oil to a 8- to 9-quart Dutch oven with a lid, set the pan over high heat, and swirl the oil in the pan. When it just begins to smoke, cook the meatballs in batches to avoid crowding, turning them occasionally with tongs, so they develop a beautiful, shiny, deep-brown crust on all sides. You don't want to cook them too fast. If you see any black spots, turn your heat down a little. Keep at it until you're happy with the color of each one, transferring them to a plate when they finish browning. It'll take 12 to 15 minutes per batch. Drain half the fat remaining in the pot.

Make the sauce: Lower the heat to medium-high, add the onion, garlic, and salt, and cook, stirring often, until the onion is soft and lightly browned and the garlic smells toasty and is a deep golden brown, about 5 minutes. Add the coriander, cumin, and chilies and cook for a minute, stirring constantly.

Turn the heat to low, add the tomatoes, and simmer gently until the tomatoes begin to stick to the bottom of the pot, about 10 minutes.

Add 4 cups water and raise the heat to bring the sauce to a boil, then turn it down to maintain a gentle simmer and cook for 5 minutes more. Transfer 2 cups of the sauce to a blender, give it a whiz until it's smooth and airy, and stir it back into the sauce in the pot. (I always freak out at this point, because the sauce seems so bland, but don't worry—it'll taste amazing after you're done.)

Return the meatballs and their juices to the pot and stir gently to coat them in the sauce. Cover the pot, tweak the heat if need be to maintain a gentle simmer, and cook for about 30 minutes to let the flavors come together.

Finish the dish: Turn the heat to low, add blobs of the yogurt, and crack the eggs here and there into the sauce. Tear and sprinkle in the mint leaves and cilantro, and add a good drizzle of olive oil. Cover the pot and turn the heat to medium. Cook until the egg whites have just set (I like my yolks a little runny), 10 to 15 minutes.

Eat it right away, from the pot or divided among shallow bowls, making sure everyone gets an egg and some yogurt.

LAMB CHOPS WITH CHIMICHURRI

When I get my hands on really good lamb, I barely do a thing to it. Why get in the way of such lovely meat? Lamb is wonderful, tender, and just a bit gamy (although you may think I'm a nutter for saying this, sometimes I think lamb tastes almost marshy), but there are two little extra steps you can take to highlight what makes it so nice: First, give your chops a light whack before grilling, just to flatten them a bit so there's even more surface area to take on the salt and the char as they cook. Second, serve the chops with chimichurri sauce—its brightness and herbaciousness perfectly offsets the chops' smoky char. The result is more or less what Italians call *scottadito*, or "burn your fingers," because the chops are so delicious that you won't be able to wait for them to cool before picking them up by the bone. Please don't avoid the salty fat that rims the meat—that's the best bit.

Try them with Roasted Tomatoes and Marinated Roasted Peppers (see recipe, page 219). **serves 4**

12 frenched rib lamb chops (about 2¼ pounds)
Kosher salt
Chimichurri (see recipe, page 292)
½ lemon, if you'd like

One at a time, put the chops on three layers of plastic wrap, fold the plastic over the chops, and use a heavy pan or mallet to lightly whack the meaty portion to an even thickness of about ½ inch.

Preheat your grill to high (preferably, build a charcoal fire and let the coals turn pale gray) or heat a cast-iron griddle over high heat. Let the grates or griddle get good and hot.

Generously season the chops all over with salt. Working in batches if need be, cook the chops, turning them over once, until the exterior is deep brown and the fat is golden, just about a minute or two per side. I like them medium, pink all the way through. Arrange them nicely on a platter.

Stir the chimichurri well, have a taste, and add a little more lemon juice, if you'd like. The extra brightness is nice with the lamb. Drizzle some on each chop and eat right away.

a little lamb

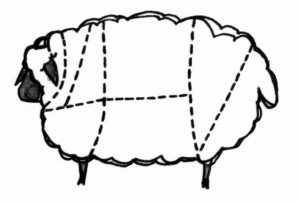

Both of my older sisters went to cooking school. I thought if I tried it and it didn't work out, at least I'd be able to make a rack of lamb—it's one of my favorite things in the world. I love the salty, crunchy fat cap, and the soft, silky, rare eye of the meat. But rack of lamb is a bit pricey. In England, a cheap substitute that still has the right amount of fat and potential for tenderness is the chump, the bit between the saddle and the leg, similar to the rump cut in the U.S. I fry it in a pan like a duck breast (slowly, to render the fat and get the meat crispy), then flip it and cook for a minute on the other side to achieve that perfect medium-rare.

My nan was always cooking up chops. I don't think there's anything better than chomping on caramelized chops, the fat dribbling down your chin, the salt sticking to your lips—like a lollipop for grown-ups. I love that the flesh comes away with a tug from your teeth. Lamb has a more complex flavor than beef. It's slightly mineral, a bit gamy, and if you've ever heard a chef call meat sweet and didn't quite understand what that meant, a bite of the chop will show you. My mom would chomp on the spinal cord attached to the chop, and suck the bones loudly.

Nan served lamb with mint sauce. I still love the way the herb interacts with lamb. It's also nice with springy ingredients, like peas and artichokes, or, in the summer, with red pepper and eggplant. In the winter, I look to garlic, rosemary, and red wine. The one constant in my lamb dishes is something acidic to counteract that gamy flavor, whether it's vinegar or red wine, tomatoes, or salsa verde.

BRAISED LAMB SHOULDER WITH TOMATO, CITRUS AND ANCHOVY

This is not some sort of misguided version of surf and turf. Anchovies, like Parmesan and soy sauce, are full of umami, and just a few lend the lamb's braising liquid an amazing saltiness and depth. The little fish melt right into the tomatoes and garlic, the carrots and wine and citrus zest, so your mates might not realize that they're even in there—but everyone would miss them if they weren't.

Shred any leftover meat and toss it and the sauce with pasta.   **serves 4 to 6**

½ cup extra virgin olive oil

1 bone-in lamb shoulder (about 6 pounds),
neck and rib bones removed

1 tablespoon kosher salt

3 medium carrots, peeled and cut into ½-inch pieces

2 Dutch or other spicy long red chilies,
pierced with a sharp knife

4 small celery stalks, cut into ½-inch pieces

1 garlic head, cloves separated, but not peeled

1 large Spanish onion, peeled and cut into ½-inch pieces

1 blood orange or small regular orange

1 lemon

1 tablespoon rosemary leaves, roughly chopped

One 28-ounce can peeled whole tomatoes, drained, trimmed,
and squished with your hands

4 whole salt-packed anchovies, rinsed, soaked, and filleted
(see Filleting Salt-Packed Anchovies, page 10)

About 1½ cups dry white wine, such as Sauvignon Blanc

Find a Dutch oven large enough (about 6 or 7 quarts) to hold the lamb shoulder with a little room to spare. Add the olive oil to the pot and set it over high heat until the oil begins to smoke. Season the shoulder all over with the salt and carefully add it to the smoking oil, fatty side down. Brown it all over, using a spoon to occasionally baste it with the hot fat. It'll take at least 15 minutes to achieve a deep-brown color, which is essential to bringing out the lamb's sweetness and giving the dish a rich flavor. When it looks beautiful, move the shoulder to a plate and set aside for the moment. Discard half the fat in the pot.

Turn the heat down to medium, add the carrots to the pot first, then add the chilies, celery, garlic, and onions, but don't stir them. You want to let them steam on top of the carrots for a bit until the carrots start to brown slightly. Cook for 10 minutes, then give all the vegetables a good stir and cook them, stirring occasionally to keep them from sticking to the pot, until they're all softening and browning a bit, about 15 minutes more.

Meanwhile, preheat the oven to 400°F.

Use a peeler to cut five long ½-inch-wide strips of skin from the orange and then from the lemon, then cut away the white pith from the strips. Add the citrus skin, rosemary, tomatoes, and anchovies to the pot and cook for 5 minutes, stirring so all the flavors have a chance to marry. Squeeze in the juice of the orange and half the lemon, and give a stir. Return the shoulder to the pot and pour the wine and 1½ cups water around, not over, it. Raise the heat slightly to bring the liquid to a simmer.

Cover the pot and put it in the oven. After 30 minutes, lower the heat to 300°F and cook, rotating the pot once halfway through, basting the shoulder with the pan liquid every half an hour or so (I also like to pile some of the vegetables on top of the meat), and removing the lid 30 minutes or so before the lamb is ready, until the shoulder has gone melty and so tender you can easily twist off the meat with a fork, about 3½ hours. Let the lamb rest for 10 minutes, then spoon off the fat (there will be about ½ cup) that rises to the surface of the sauce. Season the sauce with salt to taste.

Haul the pot to the table, along with tongs for the meat and a spoon for the sauce, and serve.

MY CURRY

Along with lots of bubble and squeak and roast dinners, my life in England was filled with curry. Birmingham, where I grew up, has a huge Indian population. It's supposedly the place where *balti* was born, a lovely curry named for the pot it's cooked in. Curry tastes especially fantastic with a beer in the wee hours after a night of clubbing. Nothing sets you right like a good spicy curry. This is the one I make for myself—it definitely has heat, but the best part is how well the different spices get on together. It's not traditional by any means, but I really like it. Don't forget the Boiled Rice (see recipe, page 251). **serves 4**

FOR THE CURRY

1 tablespoon fennel seeds, toasted (see Spices, page 9)

2 tablespoons cumin seeds, toasted (see Spices, page 9)

1 tablespoon fenugreek seeds, toasted (see Spices, page 9)

10 whole cloves

2 whole star anise

3 green cardamom pods

3 fresh kaffir lime leaves

1 tablespoon crumbled dried pequin chilies or red pepper flakes

½ teaspoon freshly grated nutmeg

2 teaspoons ground turmeric

⅓ cup extra virgin olive oil

2 cups thinly sliced shallots

4 garlic cloves, thinly sliced

½ small cinnamon stick

½ cup finely chopped fresh ginger (from a 3-ounce piece)

3 cups drained, trimmed, and chopped canned peeled whole tomatoes

2 tablespoons Maldon or another flaky sea salt

8 cilantro roots with 2 inches of stem attached, washed well and finely chopped

A 5-inch strip of orange peel, any white pith cut away

A 5-inch strip of lemon peel, any white pith cut away

¼ cup freshly squeezed orange juice

2 tablespoons freshly squeezed lemon juice

1 tablespoon freshly squeezed lime juice

1½ cups pineapple juice (fresh, bottled, or canned)

Note:
Don't let the long ingredient list scare you off; this curry is easy to make. The only time-consuming part is collecting all the spices. If you'd like, you can start the recipe the day before you plan to serve it. Stop just before you brown the lamb and pick up again the next day.

a little lamb **169**

2 tablespoons extra virgin olive oil
4 pounds boneless lamb shoulder, cut into 2-inch pieces
2 tablespoons Maldon or another flaky sea salt

Make the curry: Combine the toasted spices, cloves, star anise, cardamom, lime leaves, red pepper flakes, nutmeg, and turmeric in a spice grinder or clean coffee grinder, and grind them until you have a very fine powder.

Heat a large Dutch oven or other heavy ovenproof pot over medium-high heat and add the olive oil. When the oil just begins to smoke, add the shallots and garlic and cook, stirring often, until they're deep brown, about 10 minutes. Add the ground spice mixture, cinnamon stick, and ginger and cook, stirring constantly, for 3 minutes. Stir in the tomatoes and salt and cook, stirring frequently, until most of the liquid has evaporated and the mixture looks quite dry, about 15 minutes.

Stir in the cilantro, citrus peel and juice, and pineapple juice, then remove from the heat and set aside.

Brown the lamb: Add the olive oil to a large skillet and set it over high heat. Season the lamb with the salt. Once the oil begins to smoke, carefully add the lamb, in batches to avoid crowding the pan, and cook, turning the pieces occasionally, until each one is nice and brown, 12 to 15 minutes per batch. As the pieces finish browning, use a slotted spoon to transfer them to the Dutch oven with the curry mixture. Brown the following batches in all the nice fat remaining in the pan, transferring the pieces to the Dutch oven as they are done, and then discard the fat.

Meanwhile, preheat the oven to 350°F.

Finish the dish: Give the lamb pieces a good stir to coat them in the curry mixture, cover the pot, and put in the oven. Cook the lamb for 1½ hours, stirring now and then.

Reduce the heat to 250°F and let it go until the lamb is fork-tender but not totally falling apart, another hour or so.

fine swine

CABBAGE AND BACON

The further into this dish you get, the more delicious it becomes. The cabbage and carrots are sweet, the shallots are creamy, and the salty, smoky bacon is tender but still has texture—it isn't falling apart. It's all swimming in rich pan liquor braced with a hit of acidic still-slightly-raw wine. I like the way it cuts through the rich bacon. The parsley at the end and a hint of juniper give the dish even more brightness. Considering it's cabbage and bacon, it's quite light—hearty but not overly heavy. I love my bowl topped with a dollop of melting horseradish-infused crème fraîche with bread on the side.

It all goes really well with hot boiled potatoes tossed in lots of butter and black pepper. You can even make it the day before and warm it gently when you're ready to serve it.

serves 4

¼ cup extra virgin olive oil

A scant 1 pound skinned slab bacon, cut into slices
approximately ½ inch thick and 3½ inches long

10 medium shallots, peeled and root end trimmed but kept intact

2 medium carrots, peeled and halved crosswise

1 small savoy cabbage (about 2 pounds), outer leaves removed,
quartered through the core

1 head garlic, cloves separated but not peeled

3 tablespoons unsalted butter, cut into chunks

5 large juniper berries

1 teaspoon finely chopped rosemary

1 teaspoon Maldon or another flaky sea salt

½ cup dry white wine, such as Sauvignon Blanc

2 cups Sticky Chicken Stock (see recipe, page 302), gently warmed

¼ cup roughly chopped flat-leaf parsley

About ½ cup Horseradish Sauce (see recipe, page 295; optional)

Preheat the oven to 400°F.

Pour 2 tablespoons of the olive oil into a heavy-bottomed roasting pan or wide cast-iron skillet and set it over high heat, straddling two burners if you have to. When the oil ripples and just begins to smoke, add the bacon pieces in one layer and

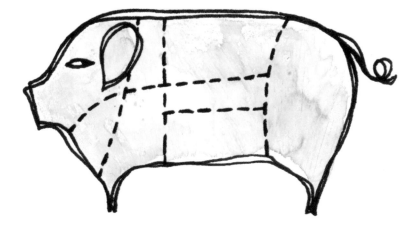

cook until they begin to release a little fat and brown on the bottom, about 4 minutes. As you cook, turn the pan occasionally to distribute the heat evenly.

Turn the bacon over and cook until golden brown on both sides, about 4 minutes more. Remove the bacon slices and set them aside on a plate. Add the shallots and carrots, and once the carrots begin to brown, about 2 minutes, reduce the heat to medium. Add the cabbage wedges to the pan, cut side down. Then add the garlic cloves and butter pieces, scattering them around the pan. Cook the cabbage, peeking underneath the wedges occasionally to make sure they're browning steadily. If they're not browning after 6 minutes, turn the heat up slightly. Once the cabbage is nice and brown on the bottom, about 12 minutes, carefully turn the wedges over onto the other cut side and sprinkle the juniper, rosemary, and salt over the vegetables. Return the bacon to the pan, tucking it in the spaces between the cabbage wedges, along with any fat that has collected on the plate. After another couple of minutes, add the wine and stock to the pan and turn off the heat.

Cover the pan tightly with foil and pop it into the oven. Cook for 25 minutes, then baste the cabbage and bacon with the pan juices. Cover the pan again and continue to cook until the carrots and cabbage are tender, about 20 minutes.

Baste the cabbage and bacon once more, season with salt to taste (depending on the saltiness of the bacon, you may add a generous amount or none at all), drizzle on the remaining 2 tablespoons olive oil, and sprinkle on the parsley. Serve with the sauce alongside.

SAUSAGE-STUFFED ONIONS

Each year that I worked at The River Café, Ruth and Rose took some of the staff on a trip to a different region of Italy. One of the trips was to Piemonte, where we spent a few days in Bra, the city where the Slow Food movement was born. The food was wonderful, of course, but it began to feel like every dish we ate contained the same local sausage. By the end of the trip, we were a bit sausaged out. At our last dinner in Bra, the waiter brought out a big roasted onion standing on a plate, and we all started nudging each other, joking that even this would be stuffed with sausage. In heavily accented English, our waiter described the dish. We giggled like kids when he told us what was inside. Good thing, then, that it was really tasty.   **serves 4**

4 medium red onions (about 8 ounces each), peeled,
stem ends trimmed, root ends trimmed but left intact

About 3 tablespoons extra virgin olive oil

Maldon or another flaky sea salt

1 head garlic

A small handful of small thyme sprigs, plus 1 teaspoon leaves

½ cup Italian sausage, homemade (see recipe, page 181)
or store-bought (removed from casing if necessary)

1 cup heavy cream

Preheat the oven to 400°F.

Put the onions in a medium Dutch oven or other ovenproof pot with a lid. Drizzle some olive oil into your hand and rub it onto the onions. You'll probably end up using about 2 tablespoons. Grab some salt and crush it between your fingers as you sprinkle it all over each onion, turning the onions to make sure the salt adheres to all sides. Put them in the pot.

Tear off the outermost layers of peel from the garlic head so the cloves are exposed. Put it in the middle of the onions and drizzle on a little olive oil. Scatter the thyme sprigs over the onions, and pour ⅓ cup water around the onions and garlic.

Cover the pot and put it in the oven. Cook just until the onions are lightly browned and soft enough that you can insert a knife into the center with barely any resistance, 50 minutes to 1 hour, depending on the size of your onions. Let them sit, covered, on the top of the stove until they're cool enough to handle, so they get even softer. (Leave the oven on.)

Carefully transfer the onions to a plate or cutting board, leaving the liquid behind in the pot. Use a small spoon to scoop out a few layers of the insides of each onion, and stuff each one with about 2 tablespoons of the sausage. Add the scooped-out onion bits to a 12-inch ovenproof pan or small baking dish. (When you add the cream and water, the liquid should come a little less than halfway up the sides of the onions.) Squeeze the soft flesh of the garlic cloves into the pan, and add the thyme leaves, cream, 1 cup of water, and 1 teaspoon salt. Bring the mixture to a full boil, add the stuffed onions, sausage side up, and baste them with the liquid for a minute or so.

Pop the pan into the oven, uncovered, and cook, basting the onions every 10 minutes or so, until the sauce is thick but not gloopy, about 40 minutes. Taste the sauce and add a little more salt, if you'd like. Bring the pan to the table, spoon a little of the sauce over the top of each onion, and dig in.

fine swine

CASSOULET

There are a lot of lovely things hiding in this one-pot meal—juicy sausage, luscious duck confit, tender lamb neck, and sticky pork skin—but the dish still tastes bright from the wine and tomatoes and crunchy, herby bread crumbs. As much as I adore all that flesh, I'm really mad about the beans, creamy and full of flavor.

You don't make cassoulet in a day. It's a leisurely process, happily spread out over several. You can make the duck confit up to a few weeks earlier. Two days before dinner, soak the beans, then cook them and refrigerate until the next day. The day of, there's just 30 minutes of active cooking. **serves 6 to 8**

1 tablespoon extra virgin olive oil

1 pound bone-in lamb neck
(cut into 2-inch-thick slices by your butcher)

Kosher salt

½ pound skinned slab bacon, cut into 4 large chunks

½ medium Spanish onion, halved

1 medium fennel bulb, stalks, fronds, and tough outer layer removed,
bulb cut into large pieces

1 small carrot, peeled and cut into large pieces

1 small celery stalk, cut into large pieces

6 ounces pork skin, fat removed by your butcher,
rolled into a bundle and tied with butcher's twine

2½ cups Sticky Chicken Stock (see recipe, page 302)

1½ cups dry white wine, such as Sauvignon Blanc

1 cup drained, trimmed, and chopped
canned peeled whole tomatoes

1¼ cups dried cannellini beans, rinsed, picked over,
soaked overnight in water, and drained

Maldon or another flaky sea salt

2 duck confit legs, preferably made yourself (see recipe, page 119),
with ⅓ cup duck fat or canola oil

3 raw Toulouse sausages or other garlicky sausage
(about ½ pound total)

2 tablespoons freshly squeezed lemon juice

1 giant handful of small, delicate flat-leaf parsley sprigs,
roughly chopped

2 medium garlic cloves, finely grated

1¾ cups coarse bread crumbs
(see Bread Crumbs, page 12)

Pour the olive oil into a 6- to 8-quart Dutch oven or ovenproof pot and set it over medium-high heat until the oil just begins to smoke. Season the lamb neck all over with kosher salt, and add it and the bacon to the hot oil. Cook, flipping the neck and bacon once, until they're golden brown on both sides, about 10 minutes.

Add the onion, fennel, carrot, and celery and cook, turning the vegetables occasionally, until golden brown, about 10 minutes. Add the pork skin bundle to the pot, then stir in the stock, wine, tomatoes, and beans. If the beans are not covered, add enough water to cover them. Cover the pot, let the liquid come to a simmer, and tweak the heat to maintain a very gentle simmer.

Cook, covered, for 2 hours, then use a slotted spoon to transfer the vegetables to a blender. Puree them, along with 1 cup of the cooking liquid, and pour the mixture back into the pot. Stir in 1 tablespoon sea salt, and cook, uncovered, until the beans are creamy inside and the meat is tender enough to pull easily from the bone, 2 to 3 hours longer. Remove the pot from the heat, season with sea salt to taste, and let the contents cool completely, then refrigerate overnight or for up to 2 days to let the flavors develop.

Preheat the oven to 300°F.

Gently dig into the beans and remove the lamb neck pieces. Pick off the meat in big chunks (discard the bones) and add them to the beans. Take out the pig skin bundle, discard the string, and cut the skin crosswise into 1-inch-thick slices. Gently stir them back into the beans. Set the pot over low heat.

Heat the duck fat or canola oil in a large pan over medium-high heat. Add the duck confit, skin side down, along with the sausages, and cook until the duck skin is crispy and golden brown and the sausages are golden brown and nearly cooked through, about 10 minutes. (If your pan isn't large enough, cook the duck and sausage separately.) Turn off the heat, flip the duck legs, and let them continue to cook in the residual heat of the hot pan.

Cut the sausages into 2-inch-long pieces and stir them into the beans, along with the lemon juice. Use your knife to separate the duck thighs from the drumsticks and add them both here and there to the beans, almost completely burying them.

Put the parsley and garlic in a small food processor and pulse until the parsley is finely chopped. Add the bread crumbs and pulse until they're fine and green.

Once the fat in the pan has cooled a bit, add ¼ cup of it (reserve the rest for the moment) and pulse until you have a rough puree. Stir in a good pinch of sea salt.

Scatter half the bread crumb mixture over the surface of the cassoulet and bake for 20 minutes. Drizzle about 2 tablespoons of the duck fat remaining in the pan over the crumbs and bake for 20 minutes more.

Scatter the remaining bread crumbs over the cassoulet and bake until the crumbs are lightly golden and crispy, about 15 minutes more.

Serve the cassoulet from the pot at the table.

SIMPLE SAUSAGE

I love stuffing sausage into casings and forming little links, and you can do the same, if you'd like. But to keep things simple, I've given you a loose sausage mix, which you can form into patties (for a lovely breakfast sausage, just leave out the fennel and chilies) and brown in a pan. Or try tossing browned chunks with orecchiette and broccoli rabe, or use it to make Sausage-Stuffed Onions (see recipe, page 174). **makes 2½ pounds**

1½ pounds boneless pork shoulder, cut into 1-inch pieces
1 pound pork fatback, cut into 1-inch pieces
2 tablespoons kosher salt
½ nutmeg, grated
2 teaspoons fennel seeds, ground
10 dried pequin chilies, crumbled, or pinches of red pepper flakes

Special Equipment
Meat grinder or meat grinder attachment of a stand mixer

Combine the shoulder and fatback in a large mixing bowl and toss well. Cover the bowl with plastic wrap and pop it in the freezer until the edges of the meat get crunchy, about 1 hour.

Use a meat grinder (or the grinder attachment of a stand mixer) to grind the mixture through a large die into a bowl.

Add the salt, nutmeg, fennel, and chilies, then mix with your hands, folding over and pushing down on the mixture, for a minute or two. You're trying to get the fat and meat and seasoning evenly distributed, but you're also mixing it so it gets a bit sticky. This will help the sausage stay firm and hold together.

If you'd like, make a little patty and fry it up to test the seasoning. You can add a bit more fennel, nutmeg, chili, and/or salt, if you'd like. Use it straightaway, or cover with plastic wrap and keep it in the fridge for 2 to 3 days or the freezer for up to a month.

WHOLE SUCKLING PIG

It may sound difficult, roasting a whole pig. You might imagine giant smokers or spits suspended over roaring fires. But a little pig like this one becomes a riot of juicy meat and golden-brown, cracker-crisp skin in your oven in about 3 hours. The meat is so tender that there's no carving necessary. Rather, a pair of tongs is all that's required to pull away moist, steamy chunks of meat with crispy skin attached. Score the skin and salt the pig liberally, that's all you have to do.   **serves 8 to 10**

One 12- to 15-pound suckling pig, fully dressed
and scalded to remove any hairs
½ cup kosher salt

Special Equipment
A razor blade; a large baking sheet and a large cooling rack
that fits comfortably in the pan; parchment paper

Put a rack in the lower third of the oven, remove any other racks, and preheat the oven to 350°F.

Lay your pig on its side on a work surface. Use the pointy corner of a razor blade to make long shallow diagonal slits every inch or so in the pig's skin (be careful not to cut into the flesh). Flip your pig over and repeat on the other side.

Salt the pig all over, inside and out, seasoning a little more heavily in the cavity and on fleshier parts like the hind legs. Don't neglect the face or snout. Rub the pig as you season to make sure most of the salt adheres, though, of course, some will end up on your work surface.

Put the cooling rack on the baking tray and prop the pig Sphinx-like on the rack—on its belly with its legs facing forward. Make sure it's secure and won't topple over as it cooks. It's okay if there's a little overhang. Tear off two small pieces of parchment paper and wrap them around the ears, then wrap the parchment in aluminum foil. (The parchment keeps the ears from sticking to the foil and the foil keeps the ears from burning.) Wrap the tail and snout in the same way.

Carefully transfer the tray to the oven rack and cook just until a back leg feels nice and loose when you wiggle it, about 2½ hours. Check on the pig occasionally to make sure it's slowly browning and the skin is getting crisp.

Crank the heat up to 450°F and continue cooking, checking on the pig often, until the skin is deep brown and crisp with pale, puffy patches here and there, 10 to 20 minutes more.

Haul the pig to the table, either on the baking sheet or on a giant platter or wooden board. Let it rest for 15 minutes or so. Go at it with tongs.

the not-so-nasty bits

LIVER AND ONIONS

I didn't typically fancy my mom's cooking, but she did liver and onions well. She used to dust the livers in flour and fry them up before adding stock and onions to the pan, transforming the whole mess into a stewy gravy. On weeknights, I'd be staring at the TV, still in my school uniform (my shirt wrinkly, my tie half undone), when I'd smell her cooking. Liver has this warm, sweet, inviting smell. She used to warn me that I'd get square eyes from watching too much telly. Putting the liver to sizzle was a better way of getting me to turn away.

My version is a little cleaner and not as heavy as my mom's, and the method makes it less likely that you'll overcook the liver. The pile of sweet onions served alongside complements the mineral quality that I adore in liver, cooked medium-rare to medium so its texture is a bit snappy with a touch of creaminess. A finishing drizzle of nice balsamic vinegar makes the dish pop. Turn it into a meal with a steaming-hot pile of Jerusalem Artichoke Smash (see recipe, page 242) or Mashed Potatoes (see recipe, page 235). **serves 4**

FOR THE ONIONS

¼ cup extra virgin olive oil

1 tablespoon unsalted butter

3 medium-large Spanish onions, halved lengthwise
and thinly sliced

1 tablespoon Maldon or another flaky sea salt

FOR THE LIVER

2 pounds calf's liver, cut crosswise across the lobe
into four ½-inch-thick slices (each about 8 inches long)
by you or your butcher

2 tablespoons extra virgin olive oil

Kosher salt

2 tablespoons unsalted butter

12 sage leaves

A drizzle of nice, thick balsamic vinegar

Put the olive oil, butter, and onions in a medium pot with a lid and sprinkle on the salt. Set the pan over medium heat, have a stir, and cover. Cook, stirring now and then, until the onions are tender and creamy but still have a bit of texture, about 20 minutes.

Remove the lid and turn the heat up to high. You want to get a bit of color on the onions, so first you've got to cook off some of the liquid in the pan. It'll evaporate faster if you don't stir all that often. Keep an eye on the onions, and take the pan off the heat when they've turned golden with spots of brown here and there, 10 to 15 minutes. (The onions keep covered in the fridge for up to 2 days.)

Gently pat the liver slices dry with paper towels. Pour 1 tablespoon of the olive oil into a large heavy-bottomed pan set over high heat. When it starts smoking quite a bit, season 2 of the liver slices generously on each side with salt (liver loves and needs plenty of salt), and add them to the pan. Cook, shaking the pan once, until the bottoms of the slices are deep brown, about 1 minute or so. Flip the slices and add a tablespoon of the butter to the pan. When the butter starts to froth, add 6 of the sage leaves, making sure that they're lying in the frothy butter. Cook until they're crispy, about 1 minute. Transfer the sage leaves to a paper towel to drain.

Keep cooking the liver slices for another minute or so, then flip them once more. Cook for 30 seconds to a minute more for medium-rare to medium. The inside will have faded from the deep-pink color of raw liver to a uniform color that's got just a hint of pale pink. That's how I like it. Put the slices on a large serving plate and keep it in a warm place while you cook the second 2 slices.

Pour off the fat and wipe out the pan. Add the remaining tablespoon of olive oil to the pan and heat it over high heat until it smokes, then season the slices of liver generously with salt and repeat the cooking process above, using the remaining butter and sage. Transfer the slices to the serving plate.

Discard the fat in the pan, and add the caramelized onions. Warm them through over medium heat, stirring often.

Top the liver with the crispy sage leaves, heap the onions alongside or scatter them over the liver, and add a good drizzle of balsamic over it all.

SWEETBREADS WITH
BRAISED BABY ARTICHOKES AND PROSCIUTTO

Sweetbreads have a more subtle flavor than the iron-y liver and kidneys, but their texture is what I love most about them. I like mine cooked to medium or medium-well, when they have a creamy texture and a springy chewiness. (Cook them to rare, and all you'll get is the creaminess; cook them to well-done, and you'll lose it entirely.) Simple braised artichokes draped with prosciutto bring a similar delicacy, and it all makes an elegant dish. **serves 4**

FOR THE ARTICHOKES

3 tablespoons extra virgin olive oil

9 medium garlic cloves, peeled

1 medium carrot, peeled and cut into ½-inch pieces

1 small Spanish onion, finely chopped

1 fresh bay leaf, or ½ dried

1 teaspoon Maldon or another flaky sea salt

½ cup dry white wine, such as Sauvignon Blanc

6 medium baby artichokes, trimmed and halved lengthwise
(see How to Prep Artichokes, page 61)

Five-fingered pinch of mint leaves, preferably black mint

2 thin slices prosciutto

FOR THE SWEETBREADS

2 lightly packed teaspoons rosemary leaves

2 lightly packed teaspoons thyme leaves

1 small garlic clove, chopped

1 tablespoon extra virgin olive oil, plus extra for drizzling

2 to 3 dried pequin chilies or pinches of red pepper flakes

Two 12-ounce lobes veal sweetbreads, trimmed, soaked,
and separated into pieces (see Prepping Sweetbreads, page 193)

Maldon or another flaky sea salt

½ lemon

Cook the artichokes: Find a 4- to 5-quart pot that has a lid—it should be wide enough so that when you add a cup of liquid later, it will cover the artichokes by half. Heat 3 tablespoons of olive oil in the pan over medium-high heat. When the oil just begins to smoke, turn the heat to low, add the garlic, carrot, onion, bay leaf, and salt, cover the pan, and cook, stirring occasionally, until the garlic and carrots are very tender but still keep their shape, about 10 minutes. You're not looking to get any color on the vegetables.

Remove the lid, increase the heat to medium, add the wine, and let it come to a boil. Add ½ cup water and the artichokes, cover the pan, and lower the heat to maintain a gentle simmer. Cook until the artichokes are knife-tender, about 10 minutes. Remove from the heat. (You can do this the night before you cook the sweetbreads; just warm the artichokes up again before the next step.)

Roughly chop the mint and add it to the pan. Drape the prosciutto over the artichokes, cover the pan, and leave it alone for 5 minutes or so.

Cook the sweetbreads: Preheat a grill or a cast-iron griddle over high heat until it just begins to smoke.

While it heats, very finely chop the rosemary, thyme, and garlic together on a cutting board. Pop the mixture into a medium mixing bowl. Pour in the olive oil, crumble in the chilies, and give it a good stir. Add the sweetbreads to the bowl and toss well.

Add the sweetbreads to the hot pan and cook, turning them over once, until they're deep brown on both sides and cooked to medium to medium-well (taste a piece: it should have a creamy texture with a little bouncy chewiness), about 6 to 8 minutes. Transfer the sweetbreads to a serving plate and let them rest for a couple of minutes, then season them generously with salt and lightly with lemon juice.

Arrange the artichokes on and around the sweetbreads. Spoon on the vegetables and some of the liquid, and tear and arrange the prosciutto over the artichokes however you'd like. Drizzle on a little olive oil and serve.

PREPPING SWEETBREADS

Sweetbreads are easy to prepare. Your butcher can remove the tough translucent membrane for you, or you can do it yourself. If you're deft with a knife, simply trim off the membrane. Or pop the sweetbreads into a large pot of boiling salted water for 3 minutes (if you do this, don't cook them for quite as long later on), then run them under cold water. You'll be able to pull the membrane off with your fingers.

Next, put the sweetbreads in a bowl and set it under cold running water, letting the water overflow, until their reddish color has become pale pink, about 10 minutes. Use your fingers to gently separate the lobes into smaller pieces of whatever size you'd like. I use pieces that are about as long as a finger and as wide as the width of three fingers. Pat the sweetbreads dry with paper towels before cooking.

not so nasty at all

My granddad never did travel light. Whenever we went on holiday, whether it was a car ride to Devon or a plane trip to Portugal, he'd bring some kidneys with him in a cooler. My nan also packed a heavy bag, but hers was filled with bottles of gin. On these trips, Granddad would fry up the kidneys for breakfast, maybe with some eggs and tomatoes. I loved them. They tasted warm and inviting and had a smell, as if umami was floating around in the air, which made you want to dig in right away. Granddad would eat them slowly, the way he ate everything, chewing really well. Nan covered hers in black pepper, because she covered everything in black pepper.

Not only do most people not haul kidneys around in their suitcases, they also don't care much for them at all. Same goes for other offal, like liver and sweetbreads, and for other tasty but neglected cuts like tongue and ears and feet—all the parts that people avoid for being a little too this or too that.

I understand why the nasty bits are not that popular. Not so long ago, people ate these bits all the time, so as not to waste food. When an animal was killed, you'd make sausage from the blood, and next you'd use all the stuff that would go bad quickly—the kidneys, the liver, the stomach. But now that you can buy any cut you want at the supermarket, you no longer really need to eat offal, so people have lost the taste for it.

Another big reason goes along with the first. When people finally do give one of these bits a chance but mess them up in the cooking, the result can be horrible. My mom had a go at cooking pig's trotters once. She had them boiling for hours and hours on the stove, and when she put them down in front of me and my sisters, along with a few slices of carrot, they still looked like hooves. I remember trying to take a bite, holding a trotter with one hand and holding my nose with the other.

But, as with any part, when offal is cooked the right way, it's a beautiful thing. So I cook the so-called nasty bits (or as I prefer to think of them, the not-so-nasty bits) and serve them at my restaurants because I like them. And I cook what I like. Then there's the part of me that hopes that just maybe, by serving a perfectly sticky trotter, I'll start converting nonbelievers, as evangelists like Fergus Henderson and Mario Batali have done. I suppose these recipes count as me giving that a go.

VEAL KIDNEYS WITH GARLIC BUTTER

Kidneys are one of my favorite bits of offal—I like the way they snap in your mouth when they're medium-rare, a bit like peas, and they remind me of my childhood and of my granddad. They have this smell when they're in a hot pan, a sort of crispy, inviting aroma that only a few other things—foie gras, squid, mushrooms—have. Kidneys are so nice with mustard or peas and bacon or cream. But this might be my favorite way to eat them. Try them over piping-hot Soft Polenta (see recipe, page 248) or Mashed Potatoes (see recipe, page 235).   **serves 4**

2 pounds veal kidneys
¼ cup extra virgin olive oil
3 large garlic cloves, finely chopped
5 tablespoons unsalted butter, at room temperature
A handful of small, delicate flat-leaf parsley sprigs, roughly chopped
Maldon or another flaky sea salt
½ lemon

Trim off as much white fat from the kidneys as you can and cut them into pieces about the size of small lemons. Trim off any more fat you spot, then cut the pieces crosswise into ½-inch-thick slices.

Heat 1 tablespoon of the olive oil in a large pan over high heat until it begins to smoke. Add about a quarter of the kidney slices to the pan (you'll have to cook the kidneys in batches so as not to crowd the pan) and let them sizzle away for a minute or so without shaking the pan. You're just getting them started and putting a bit of golden-brown color on them. Have a sniff, because it's a great smell. When some spots are a nice golden color but you still see plenty of uncooked spots on the kidneys, pour the pan's contents, kidneys, oil, and all, into a colander set over a bowl, and let the oil and some of the juice drain off while you cook the next lot. Repeat the process with the remaining kidney slices, adding another tablespoon of oil for each batch and wiping the pot clean with a damp towel if any bits stuck to the pan get too dark.

Pop the pan back over high heat, add the garlic, and cook it in the slick of residual oil, stirring occasionally, until it just begins to go golden, about 1 minute.

Add the butter, letting it melt and froth as you swirl the pan a bit. Add the whole lot of kidneys back to the pan and toss in the parsley. Stir a few times, then season generously with salt. The kidneys need only a minute or so in the butter—you'll still see a few pink, rare patches—to get them to medium-rare to medium the way I like them. Any further than medium and they'll be dry.

Take the pan off the heat and squeeze the lemon over the top. You don't want it lemony, you just want to add a bit of brightness. Have a taste and season with more salt and lemon, if you fancy.

Serve from the pan at the table, or spoon the kidneys and their sauce over plates of polenta or mashed potatoes.

WHY I DON'T SOAK KIDNEYS

A lot of people soak kidneys before cooking them. Not only that, some people think you're a bit nasty if you don't. After all, the English call them "pissers" for a reason. But I quite like the metallic, iron-like character of kidneys that fans of soaking seem to want to snuff out. I think if you soak your kidneys, you probably don't like kidneys all that much.

FAGGOTS

This dish, little caul-fat-wrapped packages traditionally filled with lots of pork offal, is from Black Country, the once heavily polluted area dotted with coal mines and steel mills near my hometown of Birmingham. Growing up, I used to eat faggots all the time. They were nothing special—sold in the freezer section of the local Sainsbury's under the unappealing name "Mr. Brain's Faggots." In my version, I trade the traditional offal-heavy filling for one of luscious braised pork cheeks that have been mixed with just a bit of pig's liver to fortify the porky flavor.

I have a bit of a giggle watching customers at the Pig squirm at the name, an old-fashioned term meaning "bundle" where I'm from. The word definitely doesn't mean what it does in the States. In what became a classic tale among staff, a couple came in one night and ordered faggots. I think they were embarrassed about saying it, so they pronounced it as if it were a French word, as if it rhymed with "ago." Say it loud and proud, or under your breath, but make sure you try them, perhaps alongside Mashed Potatoes (see recipe, page 235), Jerusalem Artichoke Smash (see recipe, page 242), Swiss Chard with Olive Oil (see recipe, page 220), or simple braised peas.

serves 4

FOR THE CHEEKS

1½ pounds pork cheeks, trimmed of excess fat

About 1 teaspoon kosher salt

3 tablespoons extra virgin olive oil

½ pound medium shallots, halved lengthwise and thinly sliced

3 large garlic cloves, halved lengthwise and thinly sliced

1 teaspoon thyme leaves

1 fresh bay leaf, or ½ dried

1 medium carrot, peeled and finely chopped

1 teaspoon Four Spice (see recipe, page 202)

3 cups Sticky Chicken Stock (see recipe, page 302)

½ cup dry white wine, such as Sauvignon Blanc

TO FINISH THE FAGGOTS

¼ cup farro

3 tablespoons extra virgin olive oil

¼ pound pork or chicken liver, cut into 1-inch chunks

the not-so-nasty bits **199**

A small handful of small, delicate flat-leaf parsley sprigs
1 tablespoon thyme leaves
1 teaspoon Maldon or another flaky sea salt
Freshly ground black pepper
1 pound caul fat, thawed if frozen (see A Note on Caul Fat, page 201)
1 tablespoon cold unsalted butter

The day before you plan to serve the faggots: Season the cheeks all over with the salt. Set a medium sauté pan over medium-high heat and add the olive oil. Once the oil is smoking, add the cheeks—in batches if necessary to avoid crowding the pan, though once they shrink up a bit, you can probably fit in a few more—and cook them, turning them over now and then, until they're dark golden brown on both sides, about 10 minutes. As they finish, put them on a plate and set aside.

When all the cheeks have been browned, add the shallots, garlic, thyme, and bay leaf to the oil remaining in the pan (you might need to add an extra glug) and cook, stirring frequently, until the shallots and garlic have begun to brown and sweeten, about 3 minutes. Add the carrot and cook, stirring and scraping the pan to get at all those nice, sticky bits, until golden brown and sweet, 10 to 15 minutes.

Add the four spice and cook, stirring, for a minute or so. Put the cheeks back into the pan and add the stock and wine. Cover the pan and bring the liquid to a simmer over medium heat, then turn the heat to low and cook the cheeks at a gentle but steady simmer until they're spoon-tender, about 1 hour and 45 minutes. Take the pan off the heat and let the cheeks cool a bit, then transfer them, and the liquid, to a container, and pop into the fridge overnight.

The day you plan to serve the faggots: Combine the farro with 1½ cups water in a small pot and set it over medium heat. Let it come to a boil, then turn the heat to low and cook the farro at a very gentle simmer until it's tender but still has a nice chew, about 20 minutes, adding a little more water as necessary to keep the farro covered. Drain the farro and set aside.

While the farro cooks, pour 1 tablespoon of the olive oil into a medium pan and set it over medium-high heat. When the oil begins to smoke, add the liver and toss and stir until it starts to brown, about 2 minutes. The pieces should be medium-rare. Scoop the liver onto a cutting board and chop it into a coarse mush.

Remove the cheek meat from the gelatinous liquid and break the cheeks into roughly ¾-inch pieces. Combine the cheeks, chopped liver, and a packed ½ cup of the cooked farro in a large bowl. (If there's any farro left over, munch on it.) Finely chop the parsley and add it to the bowl, along with the thyme, ½ cup of the cheek broth, 1 tablespoon olive oil, the salt, and a couple twists of black pepper. Toss the mixture together until everything's well distributed, then pop it into the fridge for 20 to 30 minutes to let it firm up a bit.

Preheat the oven to 400°F. Put the remaining cheek broth in a medium pot, bring to a boil, and turn off the heat.

Remove the meat mixture from the fridge. Use your hands to form the mixture into 8 equal balls. Grab a large squareish piece of caul fat that doesn't have any big tears and lay it flat on your counter or cutting board. Place one of the balls about 1 inch from the corner, fold the corner over the ball, and roll the ball over two or three times. Trim off the excess caul fat, and tuck the loose edges underneath the ball to make a neat, tight package. Repeat with the rest of the balls. You'll have some caul fat left over; reserve it for another day.

Heat the remaining tablespoon of olive oil and the butter in a large pan (nonstick is nice here, because the faggots have a tendency to stick) over high heat. When the butter starts to go brown and nutty, add the balls seam side up (work in batches, if necessary), give each one a gentle press, and cook until their bottoms have turned light golden brown and some of the caul fat has rendered, 2 or 3 minutes. Flip each one, cook for 20 seconds or so, and transfer them seam

A NOTE ON CAUL FAT

Caul fat, a transparent membrane streaked with branches of white fat, is the lining of a pig, cow, or sheep stomach. You can get it from any good butcher, though you'll probably need to call ahead. It typically comes frozen and you'll have to defrost it in warm water so it doesn't tear when you separate it into sheets. For this recipe, buying a whole pound will ensure you'll have enough nice, intact pieces to choose from.

side down to a large baking dish or two smaller ones. (When you add the cheek broth later, it should come a quarter of the way up the side of the balls.) Make sure there's some space between the balls so you can baste them as they cook.

Pour the remaining cheek broth (there should be about 3 cups) over the balls. Pop them into the oven and cook, basting them every 10 or 15 minutes, for 40 minutes, so the faggots are warm inside, the liquid has thickened slightly, and the flavor of the faggots and the liquid have a chance to mingle.

FOUR SPICE

Four spice, a simple combination of, well, about six spices (don't ask), is fantastic with pork and great to have in your cupboard. **makes ¼ cup**

½ tablespoon white peppercorns

½ tablespoon black peppercorns

½ small cinnamon stick,
crushed with the dull side of a chef's knife

10 whole cloves

2¼ teaspoons whole allspice berries

1 small nutmeg, grated

1 teaspoon ground ginger

Put all the whole spices in a large spice grinder and grind them to a fine powder. Combine with the nutmeg and ginger in an airtight container and give it a good stir. Store in a cool, dark place for up to a month.

veg

BRUSSELS SPROUTS WITH
PANCETTA AND JUNIPER BERRIES

A really simple plate of sprouts makes me very happy, especially when they're nice and sweet. In this dish, each bite is different—in some you get a nutty, sweet nibble of garlic, in others you'll fork a sprout along with a big piece of pancetta. The juniper comes through just now and again. You might eat a sprout and not get the juniper, and you might eat another and get the juniper. I kind of like that.

The sprouts themselves shouldn't be either too soft or too crunchy. I like soft sprouts, don't get me wrong. But here I like a little crunch. It does depend on your mood, though. Some days I'll turn the heat down after they've got nice color and let them get a bit softer.

serves 4

1 pound medium Brussels sprouts
About ¼ cup extra virgin olive oil
4 large garlic cloves, halved lengthwise
2 ounces thinly sliced pancetta (about 6 slices)
1 teaspoon Maldon or another flaky sea salt
About 3 dried pequin chilies or pinches of red pepper flakes (optional)
2 juniper berries, smashed and finely chopped
1½ teaspoons thyme leaves, chopped
½ lemon

Trim off just a bit from the base of each sprout, then peel off one or two of the tougher outer layers and slice the sprouts in half through the base.

Pour 3 tablespoons of the olive oil into a large pan and set it over high heat. When you see the oil ripple, add the garlic, give the pan a shake, and watch as the garlic sizzles, turning each piece over after 30 seconds or so, until golden brown on both sides, about 1 minute. Scoop out the garlic, leaving the garlicky oil behind, and reserve the cloves on your chopping board or a plate.

Lower the heat to medium and add 3 slices of the pancetta to the pan. Once they shrink up a little, add the rest, shifting the first 3 some so they all have space in the bottom of the pan. Cook, turning them over once or twice, until they're golden brown at the edges and just threatening to crisp, about 3 minutes; I like the pieces to still be a bit floppy. Put them on paper towels to drain.

Add the Brussels sprouts, cut sides down and in one layer, to the porky, garlicky fat in the pan. Cook, using tongs to peek underneath them occasionally to make sure they're getting color. Once the bottoms are a nice dark golden brown, turn the sprouts over and keep cooking until they're as crunchy or soft as you'd like, 8 to 12 minutes in all.

Sprinkle on the salt and chilies, if you're using them, crushing them between your fingers as you do, then add the juniper and toss in the reserved garlic cloves. Toss it all together and take the pan off the heat. Sprinkle in the thyme, add a good squeeze of lemon (you want a bit of brightness, not tartness), and drizzle on about a tablespoon of olive oil. Tear the pancetta slices in half and toss them with the sprouts. Have a taste, and add more salt, another squeeze of lemon, and/or another drizzle of oil, if you'd like. I like to let them chill out for a few minutes and then eat them warm, not hot.

bubble and squeak

When I was growing up, my sisters and I often spent nights at my grandparents' house. We'd wake up in the morning and the windows would be steamy with evaporated water from the pots cramming the stove. We'd smell cabbage and sprouts (not the healthy kind, but boiled Brussels sprouts seasoned with a ton of butter), and a massive hunk of beef or pork or lamb roasting in the oven. My nan's record player would be crooning away—maybe Bing Crosby or Frank Sinatra. When we finally sat down to eat our roast lunch, a weekly English tradition, we'd get plates piled with so much food that there wasn't an inch of empty space. There were mashed potatoes *and* roast potatoes. Carrots and peas and sprouts and cabbage. The meat almost seemed like an afterthought, though I loved the slab of lamb covered with peppery onion sauce or the pork with applesauce. By the end of the long meal, I was knackered and it was almost bedtime. Even when I was little, my nan would give me a tea mixed with a nip of brandy, and I'd sleep greedily on my little cot.

The next morning, the eating would begin again when we made the treat known as bubble and squeak from the leftovers. I want to call bubble and squeak an English person's fried rice, but I worry that I'd be insulting fried rice. Maybe that's because I've seen bubble, as it's called for short, mucked up so many times. Basically, you throw the leftovers from a roast lunch—carrots, cabbage, sprouts, peas, mashed potatoes, roasted potatoes, even meat—into a bowl and give it all a squeeze with your hands. Then you make the mush into patties that you fry up in a pan, a process that apparently makes a bubbly, squeaky sound.

I've eaten bubble a thousand times, and believe it or not, there's a real art to making it. And when you do it right, it can be glorious. Instead of providing a proper recipe for a dish that's all about spontaneity, I thought I'd share my thoughts and leave you to create your own version from leftover Roasted Veg (see recipe, page 208), Mashed Potatoes (see recipe, page 235), Brussels Sprouts with Pancetta and Juniper Berries (see recipe, page 204), and any other leftovers you have.

A thoughtful composer of bubble knows that just because you *can* throw everything in doesn't mean you should. You find a balance, hopefully one in which you're able to taste each vegetable. Aim not for a mushy mush, but rather a textured mush—some of it smooth mashed potato, some of it hunks of carrots or sprouts or roasted potatoes, and the rest somewhere in between, like pieces of onion and snappy peas. Then make little balls of the mixture, add them to a hot pan of frothing butter, and give them a push with a spatula to flatten them a bit. Once they go crispy and golden at the edges, flip them.

While there are guiding principles, there are no real rules. Once a friend came over with garlicky chicken noodles she'd made the day before. I mixed them with some roasted veg and mashed potatoes I had in the fridge and made bubble, letting the noodles get crispy in the pan. How you eat bubble is up to you too, as long as you promise to wait until it cools a bit so you can actually taste what's in it. When I'm lucky enough to have time for breakfast, not just toast and tea, I'll take bubble topped with a fried egg and some sausages or griddled tomatoes alongside. When I was little, I'd dip each bite in ketchup or HP sauce. Nowadays I like it plain.

ROASTED VEG

I'm particular about my roasted vegetables. I like them evenly tender all the way through, rather than mushy inside and crispy on the edges, or raw and crunchy in the middle. The key is roasting them in nice big pieces—carrots and parsnips kept whole and fennel and onions simply halved. That way, they have plenty of time to release their sugars while the insides soften. I like to treat them a bit like meat, browning them on the stovetop before I pop them in the oven. And even though there's nothing to them but oil, garlic, and a little salt, all this finicky fuss makes for really special veg.   **serves 4**

2 large fennel bulbs, tough outer layer removed,
fronds reserved, and stalks discarded

2 small skin-on red onions, roots trimmed but left intact,
halved lengthwise

4 medium parsnips, peeled, topped, and tailed

2 medium carrots, peeled, topped, and tailed

½ cup extra virgin olive oil

Maldon or another flaky sea salt

10 or so skin-on garlic cloves

Several thyme sprigs (optional)

Sage Pesto (see recipe, page 291; optional)

Preheat the oven to 450°F.

Trim the root ends of the fennel, just to remove any brown oxidized bits, but keep the ends intact. Halve the fennel bulbs lengthwise. Ideally your parsnips and carrots will be about the same size. If the top portion of any of them is much thicker than the others, lop off this portion and halve it lengthwise.

Pour the oil into a flameproof heavy-bottomed roasting pan, shallow baking dish, or cast-iron pan large enough to hold all the vegetables comfortably in one layer. Set it over medium-high heat until the oil is nice and hot—it should ripple, crackle, and smoke a little.

Carefully add the vegetables, cut sides down for the onion and fennel, and let them sizzle away. Turn your pan every now and then if you feel that one spot's not getting hot, and peek underneath the vegetables to make sure things are looking happy. As they brown, you'll smell the sweetness as the heat brings out the vegetables' sugars. If you see too much browning too quickly, turn the heat down a bit. When the undersides are a nice golden-brown color, about 10 minutes, turn the vegetables browned sides up and turn off the heat.

Sprinkle plenty of salt, about 1 tablespoon, over the vegetables, crushing it between your fingers as you do. Don't stir, because you don't want the vegetables to lose the salt. Scatter the garlic cloves and thyme sprigs around the pan and pop it into the oven.

This next part is a bit of a balancing act. If after 15 minutes or so in the oven, you see really nice color but the insides of the vegetables are still fairly firm, turn the heat down to 350°F. Continue to cook the vegetables, turning them over now and then and being delicate with the fennel and onions so they don't fall apart, just until you can slide a knife into the vegetables without resistance, 40 to 50 minutes.

Stack the vegetables nicely on a serving plate. I like to set an onion half and a few fennel halves on the plate first, then start arranging the carrots and parsnips on top so they face this way and that. Add the rest of the veg, including the garlic cloves, and spoon on some of the sweet fat left in the pan. Add a little more salt, but only if you fancy. I like mine not very highly seasoned. Roughly chop a handful of the reserved fennel fronds and sprinkle over the top. If you're using the sage pesto, add some of it in dollops here and there.

ASPARAGUS WITH PARMESAN PUDDING AND PROSCIUTTO

I could eat asparagus by the bucketload. When it's cooked right, silky but still a bit snappy, it's the most elegant thing, the perfect finger food. (I don't care for corpulent spears or those so slim that they look like stalks of wheat.) For a different take on the time-honored combination of asparagus and Parmesan, I like to make a simple custard flavored with the king of cheese and a little spring garlic (early in its season, when the green is very tender and the bulb is small, you can finely chop it and use it in place of the garlic cloves), then serve it alongside my asparagus. I like to construct little bites that incorporate all of the elements: I'll spoon the custard onto grilled bread, pile on some crispy roasted asparagus, and top it all with slices of porky-sweet prosciutto.

serves 4

FOR THE PUDDING

¾ cup heavy cream

¼ cup whole milk

2 spring garlic cloves, or 1 small garlic clove, finely chopped

A 1-ounce chunk Parmesan, finely grated

½ teaspoon Maldon or another flaky sea salt

1 large egg

1 large egg yolk

FOR THE ASPARAGUS

1 tablespoon extra virgin olive oil, plus a few glugs

16 asparagus spears, each a little thicker than a pencil,
woody bottoms discarded

Maldon or another flaky sea salt

A very small handful of small, tender basil leaves

½ lemon (optional)

12 thin slices prosciutto

Grilled or toasted slices of rustic bread

Make the pudding: Preheat the oven to 325°F.

Combine the cream and milk in a measuring cup. Pour half of the mixture into a small pot, add the garlic, Parmesan, and salt, stir to combine, and set the pot over medium heat. Let the liquid come to a simmer and cook for 1 minute, then turn off the heat. Blend the hot mixture until it's smooth.

Combine the egg, egg yolk, and the remaining cold cream mixture in a medium bowl and whisk really well. Gradually whisk in the hot blended mixture.

Pour the mixture into a small (2-cup) gratin dish. Fold a small kitchen towel into a square, put it into a medium baking dish, and set the gratin dish on top. Pour enough hot water into the baking dish to come to about an inch from the gratin dish's rim.

Carefully put the dish in the oven and cook just until the custard has set; it should be slightly firm around the edges but still wobbly in the middle, 25 to 30 minutes. Take it out of the oven and let the custard cool in the water, then remove it. (You can refrigerate the custard overnight, if you wish. I like to serve it at room temperature.)

Make the asparagus: Heat the olive oil over medium heat in a heavy pan big enough to hold all the asparagus in one layer. When it begins to smoke, add the asparagus to the pan, lining up the spears in the same direction. The oil should crackle and sizzle a bit. Give the spears a toss with tongs, sprinkle with a good pinch of salt, and spread them out in one layer. Cook, turning the spears occasionally, until they're golden brown in spots and tender but still snappy, about 6 minutes. Give one of the spears a squeeze—it should give just a little; it shouldn't feel either very firm or mushy. Just a minute before they're done, sprinkle the basil over the asparagus and drizzle on a little more olive

WHEN BASIL TASTES LIKE SAUSAGE

The basil-asparagus combination is one I learned at The River Café. Herbs don't always act like you'd expect them to. So while this might make me sound mad, here goes: once you add the basil to the asparagus and it gets a bit crispy, it adds more than just that herbaceous flavor—it becomes meaty, almost porky. It's an elusive miracle, though, that will escape you if you cook the basil too much or not enough.

veg **213**

oil. Flip the spears with tongs and play with the basil a little, giving it time against the hot pan and then moving it back onto the asparagus. It's nice if it gets just a little crispy.

Take the pan off the heat and let the asparagus gently finish cooking in the heat of the pan, stirring now and then and sprinkling on a little more salt and maybe a splash of lemon juice, if you'd like, just until you can pick up a spear without scalding your fingers.

Serve the asparagus on a platter with the custard, prosciutto, and olive oil–lashed toasted or grilled bread alongside.

TOMATOES STEWED WITH WHITE WINE AND SAFFRON

Part of the magic of these tomatoes is that they're not stewed to mush. Rather, they're tender and soft but retain enough shape so that when you squeeze a piece against the roof of your mouth with your tongue, you get a little pop of juiciness. To that end, find yourself fresh tomatoes that are really ripe and red yet still plenty firm. I like this with Grilled Sea Bass (see recipe, page 115) and Lentil Puree (see recipe, page 243), the acidity of the slightly raw white wine cutting through the earthy heartiness of the Puy lentils. But I have no problem eating it all on its own with a crusty loaf of bread. **serves 4**

1¾ pounds firm but ripe medium tomatoes, blanched,
peeled, and cored (see Tomatoes, page 10)

4 tablespoons unsalted butter

3 medium shallots, very finely chopped

1 medium garlic clove, very finely chopped

Maldon or another flaky sea salt

¼ teaspoon saffron threads

¾ cup dry white wine, such as Sauvignon Blanc

½ lemon (optional)

Cut the tomatoes lengthwise into quarters, then cut the quarters crosswise in half. Trim off any pale, hard bits. One at a time, hold each chunk over a bowl and use your fingers to push out the juice and seeds, reserving them for another purpose.

Put a medium pot over low heat, add the butter, and let it melt and froth a little. Add the shallots and garlic, along with a generous pinch of salt. Cook until the shallots are very soft, stirring occasionally and tweaking the heat to avoid browning them at all, about 10 minutes.

Stir in the saffron and white wine, increase the heat to medium, and let the liquid come to a boil. Add the tomatoes, give it all a gentle stir, and turn the heat down to maintain a bare simmer. Cook without stirring (you don't want to break up the tomatoes) until the tomatoes are tender but not mushy, about 6 minutes.

Stir in about 1 tablespoon of salt. Have a taste and add more salt if you'd like, and a squeeze of lemon if you'd like a little more acidity. Serve straightaway in a bowl.

MARINATED ROASTED PEPPERS

I remember walking into one of Mario Batali's restaurant kitchens when I first came to New York and finding it smelled like charred bell peppers. It's such an invigorating smell, one that makes this simple dish such a pleasure to cook. After you roast the peppers, you add vinegar, oil, and just a little garlic, and somehow they all conspire to make the peppers taste even more like peppers. When you're ready to eat them, make sure to toss them in the liquid pooling at the bottom of the bowl before you layer them with Roasted Tomatoes (see recipe, page 219), scatter them over mozzarella or bruschetta, or serve them alongside anything lamby, like merguez or roasted lamb shoulder. They also turn Lentil and Chickpea Salad with Feta and Tahini (see recipe, page 78), which I actually think tastes a bit like lamb itself, into a really nice vegetarian meal. Save any leftover marinating liquid to dress your next salad. **serves 4**

2 large red bell peppers
⅛ teaspoon finely grated garlic (about 1 small clove)
3 tablespoons sherry vinegar
2 tablespoons extra virgin olive oil
1 teaspoon Maldon or another flaky sea salt
5 or so large basil leaves

Set a cast-iron griddle, grill pan, or pan over high heat and let it get nice and hot. Put the peppers on their sides on the hot surface. If it's hot enough, you should hear a little hissing. Cook them, using tongs to rotate and position each one so that all the sides, the top, and the bottom get a chance to make contact with the pan, until you see a lot of black patches separated by wrinkly, blistered skin, 20 to 25 minutes.

Put the peppers in a medium bowl and cover it tightly with plastic wrap (it shouldn't be touching the peppers). Let the peppers steam just until they're cool enough to handle, about 20 minutes.

Remove and discard the plastic wrap. Working over another bowl, pull or cut off the pepper stems, which should come away along with a cluster of seeds, and discard. Tip the opening of the peppers toward the bowl and let any liquid inside pour out. Fish out and discard any seeds in the liquid. Cut the peppers lengthwise in half on a cutting board, trim off all the pale bits inside, and wipe out the seeds. Turn the halves skin side up and scrape off the skin with the back of your knife or peel it off with your fingers. Try your best to get all of it off. But whatever you do, don't run the peppers under water—can you imagine, washing away all that flavor?

Tear the pepper pieces into irregular strips (some quite wide, some rather thin) and add them to the bowl with the pepper juice. Add the garlic and the vinegar, then massage the peppers with your hands, stirring and tossing them a bit. Next, add the olive oil and salt, crushing the salt between your fingers. Stir it all again with your hands, tossing and rubbing the peppers, until the liquid looks creamy and a little viscous. Tear the basil leaves into big pieces and stir them in.

Eat the peppers right away, when they're still a bit warm, or up to an hour or two later. You can also keep them covered in the fridge for up to 2 days. Let them come to room temperature before serving.

ROASTED TOMATOES AND MARINATED ROASTED PEPPERS

This is a Ruthie, for sure, something she used to make at The River Café as an antipasto to serve alongside soft fresh mozzarella. The key is to buy really nice tomatoes and cook them until they're a little concentrated, still plump but with their character just slightly altered by the oven heat. Then you layer them with marinated peppers, so that as you eat, the tomatoes' acidity is balanced by the aromatic sweetness of the peppers. Of course, you could just make the tomatoes, because they're fantastic by themselves— perhaps on a sandwich or with a proper English fry-up on the weekend.   **serves 4**

3 medium garlic cloves, roughly chopped

A small handful of basil leaves, roughly chopped

2 tablespoons nice, thick balsamic vinegar

¼ cup extra virgin olive oil

1 teaspoon kosher salt

5 ripe Roma (plum) tomatoes (about 1 pound), blanched,
peeled, and cored (see Tomatoes, page 10)

Marinated Roasted Peppers (see recipe, page 216), at room temperature

Preheat the oven to 300°F.

Stir together the garlic, basil, vinegar, olive oil, and salt in a large bowl until the mixture is a bit viscous. Add the tomatoes, toss gently to coat them, and let them sit for 5 minutes.

Use a slotted spoon to transfer the tomatoes to a medium baking dish (it should be just big enough to hold the tomatoes in one layer with a little room to spare). Spoon the liquid, basil, and garlic over them—I like to pile most of the garlic and basil on top of the tomatoes.

Roast the tomatoes until their flavor is concentrated and they look a little smaller than when you started, 1½ to 2 hours. Once they begin to soften, baste the tomatoes every now and again, and use the back of the spoon to gently press down on each one. You're not aiming to squash them; you just want them to leak a little juice. Remove the tomatoes from the oven and let them cool to room temperature. (You can do this several hours in advance.)

Arrange the tomatoes on a platter. Give the peppers a good stir and toss, then scatter them over the tomatoes. Spoon on some of the tasty tomato and pepper liquids.

SWISS CHARD WITH OLIVE OIL

This might be the simplest preparation of chard imaginable, yet I still can't get enough of the way it accentuates the earthiness of this green vegetable, which has a lemony quality even before you add a squeeze of citrus. I love how the leaves turn silky and creamy and I love biting into a soft chunk of stem. Part of the beauty of the preparation's simplicity is how much room it leaves for play. You could brown some garlic and pancetta in olive oil and toss in the chard right at the end, or add some olives to the greens and serve it as a little salad to accompany creamy burrata. A few bright, salty dollops of Basil Pesto (see recipe, page 291) here and there wouldn't be rubbish, either. **serves 4**

Kosher salt
2 bunches Swiss chard (about 1½ pounds)
3 tablespoons olive oil
¼ teaspoon finely grated garlic, preferably with a Microplane
½ lemon (optional)
Maldon or another flaky sea salt

Note:
Be sure to wash your chard (both the leaves and stems) really well, dunking it in several changes of water to remove any dirt or grit. It's a horrible thing, chomping on grit, like eating a peach at the beach after it's fallen into the sand.

Bring a large pot (with a lid) of water to a boil and add a few handfuls of kosher salt, until the water tastes very salty, though not quite as salty as the sea.

Meanwhile, slice the chard leaves from the stems. Trim the brownish ends from the stems and cut the stems into rustic pieces, 1 or 2 inches long. Add the stem pieces to the boiling water and stir occasionally until they're tender but still have a little crunch, about 2 minutes. Add the chard leaves, stir well to make sure they're all submerged, and pop on the lid. Let the water return to a boil, remove the lid, and cook, stirring now and then, until the stems have just lost their crunch and the leaves are tender and silky. It should take 6 to 8 minutes from the moment you added the leaves.

Drain the chard well in a colander, but don't squeeze it to buggery. Put it in a bowl, then drizzle on the olive oil and add the garlic. Toss it well with your hands, rubbing the leaves to make sure the garlic gets dispersed. If you'd like, squeeze on just enough lemon juice so that it all tastes bright, not acidic, and then sprinkle on some sea salt.

Lay the chard gently on a plate in a lovely tangle—with some air in there, not in a big, dense clump—and serve.

a girl and her pig

CRISPY FRIED VEGETABLES

I suppose you could call this *fritto misto,* an assortment of spring vegetables encased in just enough salty, crispy batter to add some textural fun but not so much that it gets in their way. The dish is about those lovely vegetables, after all. You can use whatever looks great at the market, or you can follow my lead with this combination of spring treats. The fried lemon slices, a touch bitter and tart, refresh your palate with each bite.

serves 4

FOR THE BATTER

1 cup all-purpose flour

1 cup cornstarch

1½ teaspoons baking powder

1½ teaspoons kosher salt

1 large egg yolk

About 2 cups ice-cold sparkling water

FOR THE VEGETABLES

Neutral oil, such as peanut, for deep-frying

8 baby artichokes, trimmed (see How to Prep Artichokes, page 61)

8 asparagus spears, a little thicker than a pencil, woody bottoms discarded

8 baby zucchini (each about the size of your pointer finger)

4 medium Swiss chard leaves

1 lemon, sliced into ⅛-inch-thick rounds, seeds flicked out

8 squash blossoms, stems trimmed and stamens removed

Kosher salt

TO GARNISH

A small handful of mint leaves, preferably black mint

1 lemon, cut into wedges

Special Equipment
A deep-fat thermometer if not using a deep fryer

food service

ARGO
PURE
CORN
STARCH

222

Make the batter: Combine the flour, cornstarch, baking powder, and salt in a large mixing bowl and give it a good stir. Make a well in the center of the dry ingredients and plop in the egg yolk. Whisk in the ice-cold water ¼ cup at a time, stopping when you have a smooth batter that's the consistency of heavy cream. This might take anywhere from 1½ to 2 cups water. Cover the bowl with plastic wrap and put it in the fridge until it's fully chilled, about 1 hour or up to a day before you use it.

Fry the vegetables: Pour the oil (the amount depends on your fryer's capacity) into your electric fryer and set it to 350°F, or heat at least 3 inches of oil in a Dutch oven until it registers 350°F on a deep-fat thermometer. If you're using a fryer basket, set it in the oil, just waiting for the vegetables.

Work in this order, in batches if necessary, to avoid crowding the oil, battering and frying one type of vegetable at a time: artichokes (drain and pat them dry first), asparagus, zucchini, chard, lemon, and, finally, squash blossoms. For example, begin by submerging one artichoke at a time in the batter, tapping the artichoke against the side of the bowl to ensure a light coating, and carefully adding it to the oil, then dip and add the next artichoke. Cook each batch until the vegetables are golden brown, turning them as needed and stirring delicately now and then to prevent the vegetables from sticking together or to the bottom of the basket. The artichokes, asparagus, and zucchini will take 4 to 6 minutes per batch, and the chard, lemon, and squash blossoms 2 to 3 minutes. Don't let the lemon get too many deep-brown spots. As each batch is done, transfer it to a cooling rack or paper-towel-lined tray to drain and immediately season with salt. Keep them somewhere warm, like the back of the stove, while you fry the rest.

When you've fried them all, arrange the vegetables elegantly on a platter. Finely chop the mint and sprinkle it over the top, and serve with the lemon wedges for spritzing as desired.

Note:
I suggest buying a proper electric deep fryer and fryer basket, because they're useful and quite inexpensive. Yes, you can use a Dutch oven filled with 3 inches of oil. Just don't do without a deep-fat thermometer, and keep an eye on the temperature, tweaking the heat to maintain a consistent frying temperature. Whether you have an industrial-sized deep fryer or a Dutch oven, you'll have to fry in batches. Yet this batter is so good that I've never had a problem with things going soggy. To make certain, I fry the sturdier veg first and keep them in a warm place while I fry the rest.

SUMMER SUCCOTASH

This succotash manages to feel light despite the cream content because of the under-current of acidity from the white wine and tomatoes. The sweetness of the corn, the slight crunch of the green beans, the earthiness of the zucchini, and the brightness of the tarragon and basil bring it all together. I've been known to let a steamy heap of it serve as dinner, but you'll probably find yourself piling it next to grilled lamb, smoky braised pork, or a nice charred steak.   **serves 4 to 6**

4 tablespoons unsalted butter

4 medium garlic cloves, halved lengthwise

1 medium Spanish onion, finely chopped

Maldon or another flaky sea salt

½ cup dry white wine, such as Sauvignon Blanc

2 cups heavy cream

3 cups sweet corn kernels (cut from about 4 large ears)

Kosher salt

¼ pound green beans or yellow wax beans, topped, tailed, and cut into 1-inch pieces

¼ pound small cherry tomatoes

2 tablespoons extra virgin olive oil

1 pound zucchini, cut into ½-inch-thick slices

A very small handful of tarragon leaves

A very small handful of basil leaves

1 lemon, halved (optional)

Put the butter in a wide heavy pan or pot with a lid, turn the heat to medium-high, and let the butter melt and begin to froth. Add the garlic and onion, along with a tablespoon of sea salt, have a stir, and cover the pan. Cook, stirring every now and then, for 5 minutes. Turn the heat to low and continue to cook, stirring oc-casionally, until the onions are soft and creamy but not colored, about 10 minutes more.

Remove the lid and turn the heat back up to medium-high. Pour in the wine and let it bubble away until it has almost completely evaporated, then pour in the cream and let it bubble until it has reduced by half. Add the corn kernels and cook, stirring, until they're just tender, about 4 minutes. Remove from the heat and keep somewhere warm for the moment.

Meanwhile, bring a large pot of water to a boil and add kosher salt until it's as salty as the sea. Add the beans and cook until they've just lost their raw crunch, about 3 minutes. Scoop them into a colander, drain them really well, and stir them into the corn. (Leave the water at a boil.)

Use a small sharp knife to poke each tomato just through the skin. Add the tomatoes to the boiling water, cook for 10 seconds, then transfer them to the colander. Run them under cold water, drain them well, and peel them.

Heat the olive oil in a large pan over medium-high heat until it just begins to smoke. Working in batches if necessary, add the zucchini and cook, turning over the slices every now and then, until they're just tender and golden brown on both sides, about 5 minutes. Sprinkle on a generous pinch of sea salt, then use a slotted spoon to transfer the zucchini to the pan with the corn.

Return the pan with the corn to low heat. Roughly chop the herbs and stir them into the pot. Have a taste and season with more salt and a squeeze of lemon juice, if you'd like. Serve hot.

potato
and friends

GNUDI

One day I swear I'm going to take gnudi off the menu at The Pig. We'll probably end up closing down, because it's one of the most popular items on the menu. Yet it might be worth the risk—it's been seven years of sheer hell making these little things. For cooks without a restaurant to run, though, gnudi are a dream. They're extremely simple—just a mixture of ricotta and Parmesan formed into stubby dumplings, then coated with semolina flour. They hang out in the fridge until the moisture in the ricotta has fused with the semolina to form a delicate skin. But when you must have them ready *every day* for service, it's another story. They're so temperamental—sometimes they're ready to cook after a day in the fridge, sometimes it takes two or three. I often jump the gun, cooking them too early and tearing my hair out as I watch them fall apart in the water. At home, though, there's no need to rush the process. It's easy to get right, as long as you give them three days to develop that skin—but not much longer or the skin will get too dense. In the spring, I'll occasionally leave out the brown butter and spoon Basil Pesto (see recipe, page 291) here and there.

serves 4

FOR THE GNUDI

1 pound semolina flour
1 pound sheep's-milk ricotta (see Note, page 232)
A 1-ounce chunk of Parmesan, finely grated
1 teaspoon kosher salt

TO FINISH THE DISH

7 tablespoons slightly chilled unsalted butter
20 good-sized sage leaves
Kosher salt
A handful of finely grated Parmesan

Special Equipment
Parchment paper; disposable piping bag
(or a resealable plastic bag)

Make the gnudi: Line a large baking sheet with parchment paper. Add about three-quarters of the semolina to the sheet, spreading it out to form a more or less even layer. Put the rest of the semolina in a medium bowl. Make sure there's space in your fridge to hold the baking sheet.

Combine the ricotta, Parmesan, and salt in a large bowl. Use a large wooden spoon to mash and stir the mixture until it's well combined. Put the mixture in a disposable piping bag (or resealable plastic bag). With your fingers, work the mixture toward the tip and twist the top of the bag. Use kitchen scissors to cut an opening about 1¼ inches across at the tip of the piping bag (or a bottom corner of the plastic bag). Pipe the mixture onto the semolina-lined tray in 3 or 4 long straight lines, leaving an inch or two of space between them.

Hold a pair of kitchen scissors perpendicular to the tray (you could use a knife, but the scissors make it faster and easier) and snip each strip of dough every 1¼ to 1½ inches along its length. You want to turn each strip into 9 or 10 pudgy little logs.

Working with one little log at a time, gently press the ends between your palms to make the log shorter and a little pudgier, almost round. Try not to form any creases as you do this (the gnudi shouldn't look like little bums) or any pointed edges. Hold the log gently in the palm of one hand over the bowl of semolina. Grab a large pinch of semolina and sprinkle it over the gnudi, gently turning the gnudi so the semolina coats every bit of it. Carefully return it to the semolina-covered tray, and repeat with the rest of the logs. Make sure you leave a little space between each one on the tray.

Note:
At The Pig, I use
sheep's-milk ricotta,
because I like the
gentle acidity it has.
But as long as you use
really moist, soft,
creamy ricotta, you
can get away with
using one made with
cow's milk.

Dust the semolina remaining in the bowl over the gnudi. Cover the tray tightly with plastic wrap, and pop it into the fridge. Keep the gnudi in the fridge, turning them over once a day and covering them again, until they're firm and no longer feel damp—give it at least 3 days, but no more than 4.

Cook the gnudi: Fill a large wide pan or shallow pot two-thirds full with water, salt it generously, and bring it to a boil over high heat. Meanwhile, transfer the gnudi to a large plate, giving each one a gentle but assertive shake to remove any loose semolina.

Put 3 tablespoons of the butter in a shallow pan large enough to hold the gnudi

in one layer, add ⅓ cup of the hot salted water, and set over medium heat. Once the butter has melted, take the pan off the heat.

Add the remaining 4 tablespoons butter to another large pan, set the pan over medium-high heat, and let the butter melt and foam until it goes slightly nutty and turns light golden brown. Add the sage to the butter in one layer and cook the leaves just until they've gone crispy, about 2 minutes. Transfer them to paper towels to drain and sprinkle them with salt. Keep the brown butter in a warm spot at the back of the stove, off the heat.

Ease the gnudi into the boiling water and cook, gently shaking the pot once (don't stir the gnudi), for 2 minutes. (You might want to set a timer. Don't cook them any longer, or they'll fall apart.) Set the pan with the butter-water mixture over high heat. Use a slotted spoon to quickly transfer the cooked gnudi to the butter-water and cook at a vigorous simmer, shaking the pan now and then (again, don't stir the gnudi), until the butter sauce thickens slightly and begins to cling to the gnudi, about 3 minutes.

Serve the gnudi in the pan or divide the gnudi among warm shallow bowls. Sprinkle on the Parmesan and a little salt and garnish with the sage leaves. Drizzle on as much of the brown butter as you'd like.

MASHED POTATOES

My strategy with mashed potatoes is a simple one: just when you think you've added enough butter, go ahead and add some more. I like passing them through a potato ricer for a supersmooth texture, but at home, mashing them with a whisk or masher is just fine. These potatoes go great with Liver and Onions (see recipe, page 189), Veal Kidneys with Garlic Butter (see recipe, page 196), Faggots (see recipe, page 199), or anything saucy. A nice glass of red wine too.   **serves 4**

2½ pounds Yukon Gold potatoes, peeled, halved crosswise,
and rinsed (see Potatoes, page 10)

Kosher salt

½ cup heavy cream

½ cup whole milk

½ teaspoon freshly grated nutmeg

½ pound (2 sticks) cold unsalted butter

Combine the potatoes with enough cold water to cover them by about an inch in a large pot. Add enough salt so the water tastes just a little less salty than seawater. Bring the water to a boil over high heat, then lower the heat to maintain a vigorous simmer. Cook the potatoes until you can easily poke the fattest part with a sharp knife. (Don't get poke-happy, or they'll get waterlogged.) It'll take 15 to 25 minutes total, depending on the size of your potatoes.

Drain the potatoes and let them sit in the colander for about 5 minutes; set the pot aside. The steam coming off the potatoes is evaporating water. The less water in the potatoes, the better they'll absorb the butter and cream.

Meanwhile, add the cream, milk, and nutmeg to a small pot and bring to a gentle simmer over low heat. Turn off the heat.

Return the potatoes to the warm, now-empty pot and mash them with a masher or whisk until they're as smooth as possible. Set the pot over low heat. Add a little of the milk mixture, a few tablespoons or so, stirring it in quickly and well, then add some butter, a tablespoon or two. Stir until the butter is incorporated, then add a little more of the milk mixture, and continue alternating between the butter and milk mixture until you've used them all. If you feel like your mash is getting loose, though, stop adding milk but continue adding butter. The last thing you want is runny mashed potatoes. Season with salt to taste.

the pig

A guy in New York City named Ken Friedman wanted to open a pub for himself and his friends, what would ultimately become The Spotted Pig. He was looking for a chef. I was not his first choice. Or his second.

It was 2003. I was living in London in a flat right next to my mate Pete Begg, who worked with me at The River Café. Over dinner, he told me about Ken and his pub. He said that he'd been offered the job but wasn't ready to leave London. Pete had asked Jamie Oliver, who a few years earlier was just a bloke sweating it out in the same kitchen as we were. But Jamie had turned it down too. He was already well on his way to superstardom. "Ape," Pete said, "maybe you'd want the job."

I'd been at The River Café for four years. And while I loved it there, I was ready for a change, for a new life experience. I'd never lived across the pond. I'd never eaten a slice of New York pizza or seen the Brooklyn Bridge. Pete and Jamie put in a word, so I got an interview. Ken flew me to New York and put me up at a hotel overlooking Union Square, the greenmarket full of apples and potatoes.

Turned out Ken was in cahoots with Mario Batali, whom I'd also be meeting. I had never heard of him. Now I realize that's a bit like never having heard of Jay-Z. But keep in mind that I'd spent the past decade with my head down, sautéing onions, butchering pigs, and rolling out pasta. I met the two of them at Pearl Oyster Bar, in the Village. And there was Mario in the orange clogs and red ponytail pulled back that I now know are his trademarks. I was nervous, but in a good way. As we talked, I ate a lovely cod sandwich on a crusty roll, slathered with mayonnaise.

Apparently Mario'd said something to Ken like, "If this girl's right, I'll give you the thumbs-up within the first ten minutes." To this day I'm not sure why he approved. My best guess is that at the time, I was missing a fingernail. And my arms were dotted with burns. Some of them still haven't fully faded.

Everything seemed settled until Ken sent a list of dishes he wanted on the menu. It went, "Tofu hot dogs, veggie burgers, nachos . . . ." I flipped. I sent an e-mail telling him that if that's what he was after, he had the wrong person. In a last-ditch effort to reclaim my new life, I responded with my own list, one of all the foods I was passionate about: perfectly cooked rib-eye steaks with chips and béarnaise sauce, haddock chowder, boiled potatoes with lots of butter and black pepper. I'm lucky that he trusted me. My first menu at The Pig was full of food I love. And I'm lucky that I've been able to serve that kind of food ever since.

DUCK-FAT POTATOES

With their golden, crispy crusts and creamy middles, these are lovely to serve in place of mashed or roasted potatoes. The potatoes soak up a bit of the fat and take on a subtle ducky flavor but somehow still taste clean and aren't too heavy. Turns out a lowly, inexpensive thing like the russet potato and the posh duck fat make a nice partnership. The good news is that you can use the duck fat again, as long as you strain it through a fine-mesh sieve to remove any potato bits. It'll keep in the fridge for up to a week.

serves 4

2½ pounds russet (baking) potatoes
(2 large, halved lengthwise, or 4 small), rinsed (see Potatoes, page 10)
Kosher salt
2 cups rendered duck fat, gently warmed until liquid
Maldon or another flaky sea salt

Put the potatoes in a large pot and add enough cold water to cover them by an inch or two. Add enough kosher salt so the water tastes just a little less salty than seawater. Bring the water to a boil over high heat, then lower the heat to maintain a vigorous simmer. Cook the potatoes just until you can poke the fattest part with a butter knife without much resistance. (But don't get poke-happy, or they'll get waterlogged.) It'll take 15 to 20 minutes from when they reach the boil, depending on the size of your potatoes.

Drain the potatoes well in a colander and gently shake it so the potatoes knock against its sides and get a bit fluffy and powdery looking on the outsides. It's okay if they break up a little, but you don't want them to get too crumbly. Let them sit uncovered while you heat the fat so some water escapes as steam. That way, they won't sputter and splatter when you fry them.

Preheat the oven to 450°F.

Pour the duck fat into a flameproof baking dish or deep cast-iron pan large enough to hold the potatoes in one layer with some room to spare. Set the pan over high heat until the fat begins to bubble a little, about 5 minutes. To test whether it's hot enough, gently touch one of the potatoes to the fat. It should crackle, sizzle, and bubble rapidly straightaway. (If the fat isn't hot enough when you add the potatoes, they'll stick to the pan.) When it's good and hot, gingerly add the potatoes. Cook them in the fat until they crisp up a bit on all sides and get golden at the edges, turning them over occasionally once the first side is crisp, 15 to 20 minutes.

Carefully put the pan into the oven and cook, checking on and turning the potatoes over every now and then, until they have an even deep-golden, crispy crust all over, 10 to 15 minutes.

Use a slotted spoon to transfer the potatoes to a plate, and immediately sprinkle them with sea salt, crushing it lightly between your fingers. Spoon on a little of the fat from the pan, if you fancy. I like to let them cool just a bit before I eat them.

JERUSALEM ARTICHOKE SMASH

I've got a thing for Jerusalem artichokes (also called sunchokes). They're really versatile: they're equally great raw in salads, panfried, or in a nice mash. They have a slightly sweet flavor and a nutty aroma that makes me feel good about the world. For this recipe, I like to smash them, rather than mash them, keeping them pretty chunky and adding just a bit of cream, so I don't mask their flavor. Consider these any time you're thinking of serving mashed potatoes.   **serves 4**

2 pounds Jerusalem artichokes
2 teaspoons extra virgin olive oil
1 tablespoon Maldon or another flaky sea salt
2 tablespoons heavy cream
Freshly ground black pepper
A five-fingered pinch of parsley leaves

Fill a big bowl with cold water. Peel the Jerusalem artichokes as best you can. They're a bit knobby, so it'll take some time, but it's worth it. It's okay if you can't get every last bit of skin. As you peel each one, drop it in the water to prevent browning.

Once you've peeled all the artichokes, drain them and chop them into rough 1-inch pieces. Add the pieces to a medium pot that has a lid, along with the olive oil, the salt, and ¼ cup of water. Give a good stir, cover the pot, and set it over medium-high heat. Cook at a steady simmer, stirring once in a while, until the chunks are just barely crunchy, about 25 minutes.

Take the pot off the heat. Stir and smash the chunks a bit with a sturdy whisk or spoon, then add the cream and stir and smash to incorporate it. Keep stirring and smashing until you have a rough mash, some of it smooth and creamy and some of the chokes in medium and small chunks. Add a few twists of black pepper and a sprinkle of parsley. Serve piping hot.

LENTIL PUREE

I love to use this earthy puree as a bed for grilled fish. But once you swipe a finger through it and smell its whiff of cumin and taste its subtle lemony brightness, you'll find yourself dreaming up other ways to work it into your meals, perhaps alongside lamb chops or even as a dip with toasted pita or crispy flatbread. After all, it's not so far off from hummus, is it? I often stir in a good chunk of butter at the end, and you can too, if you'd like, but it tastes sufficiently rich without it. If you serve it along with the Tomatoes Stewed with White Wine and Saffron (see recipe, page 215), a pairing I highly recommend, scale back just a bit on the lemon—the tomatoes have plenty of acidity already.   **serves 4**

½ teaspoon cumin seeds, toasted (see Spices, page 9)
1 cup heavy cream
7 medium garlic cloves, peeled
¾ cup Puy lentils, rinsed and picked over
About 3 tablespoons freshly squeezed lemon juice
1 heaping tablespoon Maldon or another flaky sea salt
2 tablespoons extra virgin olive oil

Combine the cumin, cream, garlic, and lentils with 1½ cups water in a medium pot and set it over high heat. Bring the liquid to a vigorous simmer, then turn the heat to low. Cook the lentils at a bare simmer (you don't want the liquid to reduce at all), stirring occasionally, until they're swollen, very soft, and beginning to break apart a little, about 35 minutes.

Pour it all into a blender or small food processor (work in batches, if necessary), then add the lemon juice, salt, and olive oil. Blend on low until the mixture is creamy, then blend on high until it's as smooth as possible. Have a taste. I like it when the acidity adds brightness but doesn't announce itself as lemon. Sometimes, though, I'll make it more lemony, depending on my mood, so feel free to blend in a little more lemon juice, and/or salt, if you fancy.

The puree keeps in the fridge for up to 2 days as long as you cover it with plastic wrap pressed against its surface (a layer of olive oil works too). It reheats nicely, stirred frequently, in a small pot or pan over low heat.

*Note:
At my restaurants I use a Vita-Prep blender, which is very powerful—and expensive—to blend the lentil mixture, so it's really smooth and shiny. At home, any blender will do, though a powerful blender will give you the smoothest result.*

GOAT CHEESE SOUFFLÉ

This soufflé is so easy to make that you can treat it like a starch, swapping it for polenta or mashed potatoes when you're after something lighter. The key to achieving its wonderful, airy texture is to beat the egg whites to stiff peaks, then fold them in gently, so you don't knock out too much of the air you just beat in. This soufflé is especially nice because you can let it cool, store it in the fridge, and gently reheat it the next day in a 325°F oven. It'll puff back up.

In a restaurant setting, I've served this with grilled quail, but at home I'd eat it beside a simple salad, perhaps one of sugar snap peas and sliced speck.   **serves 4**

½ cup unsalted, blanched Marcona or regular almonds

4 tablespoons unsalted butter, at room temperature,
plus extra for the baking dish

2 cups whole milk

1 teaspoon finely grated garlic, preferably with a Microplane
(about 3 medium cloves)

2 teaspoons kosher salt

A scant ½ cup all-purpose flour

½ pound fresh soft goat cheese

4 large eggs, yolks and whites separated

Special Equipment
A 1½-quart, 2-inch-high round or oval baking dish

Toast the almonds in a pan preheated over medium heat, shaking and tossing until they're a uniform golden brown, about 4 minutes. Let them cool slightly and finely grind them in a small food processor.

Preheat the oven to 350°F. Position a rack in the middle of the oven. Generously butter the baking dish. Coat the sides and bottom of the dish with an even layer of the ground almonds. Cover the dish with plastic wrap and put it in the fridge until you're ready to use it.

Combine the milk, garlic, and salt in a medium pot and bring to a boil over medium-high heat, stirring occasionally, then immediately remove from the heat and pour into a heatproof measuring cup.

Wipe out the pot, add the 4 tablespoons of butter, and set the pot over low heat.

Let the butter melt and froth a little, then add the flour, whisking until it's fully incorporated. Add the warm milk ½ cup at a time, whisking all the while until the mixture looks silky and smooth. Cook, whisking constantly, for 5 minutes, then turn off the heat. Add half the goat cheese and stir until it has completely melted. Let the mixture cool completely. Whisk in the egg yolks.

Fill a medium pot with water, bring it to a boil, and turn off the heat.

Beat the egg whites to stiff peaks in a clean stainless steel bowl, then use a stainless steel spoon to tenderly fold the whites into the goat cheese mixture. You don't want to lose too much of the air you beat into the whites by stirring too much or too roughly. It's just fine if you still see streaks of egg whites. Pour it all into the chilled soufflé dish and crumble on the remaining goat cheese in large chunks.

Line the bottom of a larger baking dish or roasting pan with a kitchen towel. Put the smaller baking dish in the center, and put it all on the oven rack. Carefully pour enough hot water into the larger dish to reach three-quarters of the way up the sides of the smaller baking dish. Bake, rotating the dish after 40 minutes, until the soufflé puffs up and there are golden-brown patches beside little crannies of white cheese, an hour or so. Let it cool in the water bath a little until you can remove the dish with your hands. Serve.

SOFT POLENTA

It's not hard to like polenta, especially when it's made with plenty of butter and cheese. But I remember the first time it went from something I found nice to have around to something I couldn't get enough of. Like so many of my food revelations, the shift happened while I was working at The River Café. I looked on as the cooks there simmered and stirred polenta for what seemed like hours. The end result was tender, textured, and slightly coarse, not a monotonous mush, and, even better, it tasted like more than just butter and Parmesan—it tasted a little sweet, like the corn it was made from. So be sure to buy high-quality polenta—Anson Mills and Cayuga Farms are fantastic sources—and prepare for some slow, steady cooking. Though it takes a while, making the polenta isn't really labor-intensive, and the final flavor is worth every minute. **serves 8**

FOR THE POLENTA

4 teaspoons kosher salt
2 cups stone-ground polenta, preferably from Anson Mills or Cayuga Farms
6 tablespoons slightly chilled unsalted butter, cut into chunks
A 1½-ounce chunk of Parmesan, finely grated

TO FINISH THE POLENTA

A few tablespoons of mascarpone
A small handful of marjoram leaves, roughly chopped
Freshly ground black pepper
Freshly grated nutmeg (optional)
Maldon or another flaky sea salt

Put 5 cups water in a medium pot, add 2 teaspoons of the kosher salt, and bring to a boil over high heat. With a heatproof whisk in one hand and a bowl of the polenta in the other, slowly and steadily pour the polenta into the boiling water, whisking as you do. Keep whisking until the polenta starts to thicken, bubble, and become one with the water, then turn the heat down to low. Leave the whisk in the pot. Tweak the heat if you need to so the polenta trembles but doesn't erupt with bubbles. Cook, stirring every now and again (you don't want to give the surface a chance to go dry) and adding a splash of water if it looks very dry, until the polenta has lost its crunchiness and is tender but not mushy. This may take anywhere from 1 to 2 hours.

When the polenta is ready, stir in the butter until it's completely incorporated, then stir in almost all of the Parmesan along with the remaining 2 teaspoons kosher salt. Keep it warm, covered, over a low heat until you're ready to eat.

Pour the polenta into a warm serving bowl. Dollop on the mascarpone and sprinkle on the marjoram. Sprinkle the pepper, nutmeg, remaining Parmesan, and a little sea salt over the top.

A TREAT FOR THE COOK

My friend Pete Begg, who cooked alongside me at The River Café, introduced me to the *crosta de caliera*, the crispy bit of polenta that clings to the bottom of the pot. He regarded it as a cook's treat, like the tender "oyster" between the chicken's leg and back. After he scooped out polenta for the customers, he'd let the pot cool slightly, until the *crosta de caliera* released its grip. He'd scrape it off, more or less in one piece, brush on some mascarpone, and sprinkle the whole thing with Parmesan and flaky sea salt. Don't neglect this snack. It's your reward for all your stirring and patience.

SIMPLE CHICKPEAS

Canned chickpeas are all right, but they're never as good as what you get when you cook the dried beans yourself. The extra step of blending the cooking liquid with the garlic and chilies that cooked with the chickpeas means your beans will be moist and flavorful. With a last-minute drizzle of olive oil, this makes a great, simple side dish.

Rose Gray had a saying about chickpeas: if they're not cooked after 25 minutes, they'll never fully cook at all. You shouldn't have to worry about this if you make sure to buy the freshest dried chickpeas you can find. **serves 4**

1 cup dried chickpeas, rinsed, picked over,
soaked overnight in water, and drained
8 medium garlic cloves, peeled
¼ cup extra virgin olive oil
2 Dutch or other spicy long red chilies, pierced with a sharp knife
1½ tablespoons Maldon or another flaky sea salt

Put the chickpeas in a medium pot with the garlic, olive oil, chilies, and 2 cups of water. (If the water doesn't cover the chickpeas by an inch or so, use another pot.) Set the pot over medium-high heat and bring the liquid to a simmer, then turn the heat down to maintain a gentle simmer. Cook until the chickpeas are just tender and a little creamy, 15 to 25 minutes. Turn off the heat, stir in the salt, and let the chickpeas cool in the liquid. Once they've cooled, they'll be even creamier.

Fish out the garlic and chilies. Scrape out the flesh and seeds from the chilies, and add them and the garlic to the blender along with ½ cup of the cooking liquid. Blend until smooth and stir the mixture into the chickpeas. The beans keep in their liquid in the fridge for several days. Gently warm them through before serving.

BOILED RICE

This simple rice is meant for My Curry (see recipe, page 169), but it's the sort of thing you'll find yourself cooking on weeknights to soak up any old saucy dish you make for dinner. Rinsing the rice in water a couple of times before cooking it removes some of the starch and keeps the grains from going gloopy.   **serves 4 to 6**

6 tablespoons unsalted butter
2 medium garlic cloves, finely chopped
1 medium Spanish onion, finely chopped
2 teaspoons kosher salt
2 cups basmati rice, rinsed twice and drained well

Put a large saucepan that has a lid over medium heat, add the butter, and swirl it around until it melts. Once it froths a bit, add the garlic and then the onion. Sprinkle on the salt, give it a stir, and cover the pan. Cook, stirring now and then, until the onion is translucent, tender, and creamy but has not colored, about 10 minutes.

Add the rice to the saucepan, give it a light stir, and then add 2¾ cups water. Raise the heat to bring the water to a strong simmer. Lower the heat to medium, cover, and cook the rice for 10 minutes, tweaking the heat if necessary so that the water doesn't either bubble over or sit there not bubbling at all. Take the pan off the heat, remove the lid, and cover the pot with a clean kitchen towel. Let the rice sit for 4 or 5 minutes, then fluff it with two forks.

Have a taste and add a little more salt, if you'd like. Serve while it's still hot and steamy.

sweets

MARINATED STRAWBERRIES

The combination of strawberries and cream is as English as the Queen. And while these simple marinated strawberries would be fantastic alongside a bowl of Devonshire or clotted cream, nowadays I like them on vanilla ice cream or folded into whipped cream and crunchy meringue crumbles for Eton Mess (see recipe, page 256). They make an intense, vibrant topping, with a touch of spice from black pepper and a sweet-tart flavor from the balsamic. Don't be wary of the booze—it's just there to pull out the flavor of the berries and make them taste even more fragrant and sweet. If you really want a treat, top the berries with ice cream, and trowel on Cornish clotted cream. **serves 4**

2 pints strawberries, rinsed, hulled, and halved if large

3 tablespoons vodka

1 tablespoon finely grated lemon zest

2 tablespoons freshly squeezed lemon juice

2 teaspoons nice, thick balsamic vinegar

Pinch of kosher salt

3 or 4 twists black pepper

¼ vanilla bean, split lengthwise

1 to 2 tablespoons sugar

Combine the strawberries, vodka, lemon zest, lemon juice, balsamic vinegar, salt, and black pepper in a large bowl. Use a knife to scrape the seeds of the vanilla bean into the bowl, and add 1 tablespoon of the sugar. Stir gently but thoroughly. Give a taste. You might need more sugar if your strawberries aren't that sweet. If you do, add it gradually, tasting as you go.

Cover the bowl with plastic wrap and pop it into the fridge. Let the mixture chill (give it an occasional stir) for at least 30 minutes, and up to an hour. The longer it sits, the more flavor the vodka will extract from the berries.

ETON MESS

My mom had strawberry plants when I was a girl, and when she wasn't looking, my sisters and I would nab the ripest berries and gather round the sugar bowl in the kitchen, dipping and biting, dipping and biting. We thought we were really clever, but my mom always spotted the traces of pink sugar we left behind. I'm not sure why we didn't just wait a bit, because those ripe strawberries would probably have ended up in Eton Mess, an English classic of fruit mixed with whipped cream and crumbles of crunchy meringue. The creation story goes that a dog sat on someone's picnic basket and squashed a pavlova. I suppose it looked like a bit of a mess, hence the name—but a pretty mess, to be sure. Strawberries are the classic, but pineapple or rhubarb or bananas would be good, wouldn't they?   **serves 4 to 6**

FOR THE MERINGUE

3 large egg whites (without a trace of yolk)
A generous ½ cup superfine sugar
Finely grated zest of ½ lemon

FOR THE WHIPPED CREAM

1 cup heavy cream
1½ teaspoons confectioners' sugar
½ vanilla bean, split lengthwise

Marinated Strawberries
(see recipe, page 255), chilled

Special Equipment
Parchment paper

Make the meringue: Preheat the oven to 200°F. (The success of the meringue relies on low oven temperature. Because some ovens aren't well calibrated, be sure to test the temperature with an oven thermometer before risking your meringue.) Line a baking sheet with parchment paper.

Fill a medium pot with an inch or so of water and bring to a boil. Use a clean whisk or rubber spatula to stir together the egg whites and sugar in a clean large stainless steel bowl. Once the water reaches a boil, turn off the heat and set the bowl of egg whites over the hot water, so the water isn't touching the bowl's bottom, and stir constantly until the sugar has completely dissolved and the mixture is white, frothy, and no longer grainy, about 8 minutes.

Remove the bowl. Use a whisk, handheld electric mixer, or stand mixer fitted with a whisk attachment to beat the egg whites on high to very stiff, shiny peaks, 4 to 5 minutes. (They should be so stiff that when you hold the whisk horizontally, the peaks stick straight out without bending.) Gently fold in the lemon zest.

Spoon the mixture into 4 equal mounds on the lined baking sheet. I like to take an extra few seconds to make sure each one is spiky. Bake the meringue until it's dry and crunchy on the outside but still soft and chewy inside, about 6 hours. Let it cool. (Stored in an airtight container lined with parchment paper, the meringues will keep for up to a day at room temperature or up to a week in the freezer.)

Make the whipped cream: Combine the cream and sugar in a large bowl. Use a knife to scrape the seeds of the vanilla bean into the bowl; discard the pod. Use a whisk or handheld electric mixer to whip the cream to semi-stiff peaks. Cover and refrigerate until ready to use.

Make the Eton Mess: Crumble the meringues into a large mixing bowl; you should have a combination of small crumbles, medium pieces, and large chunks. Add the whipped cream and stir gently just until the meringue pieces are coated. Add about three-quarters of the strawberries and their liquid and stir very gently just until the berries are well distributed but you still see streaks of red in the white cream.

Carefully scoop the mixture into a large serving bowl, scatter the remaining strawberries on top, and drizzle on the rest of the strawberry liquid. Serve straight-away.

RHUBARB FOOL WITH CARDAMOM CREAM AND PISTACHIOS

We English are always chuffed by the combination of fruit and dairy. When I was a little girl, my mom would pop open a can of peaches and douse them in evaporated milk. My sister would sit next to me, just watching as I dug in. "That'll make you fat, that will," she'd say. Later, she'd eat my leftovers.

Rhubarb is as English an ingredient as peas or strawberries, and fool is a classic dessert as close to any Brit's heart as trifle. I made many a fool as a young cook in England. The rhubarb's earthy flavor and sharp tartness balance the floral cardamom whipped cream. I layer the fool in small clear jars, so you can see the pink and white, pink and white. Well-chilled, it's wonderfully refreshing. And not too sweet.

serves 4

FOR THE CARDAMOM CREAM

6 green cardamom pods

3 tablespoons superfine sugar

1 cup crème fraîche

1 cup heavy cream

FOR THE RHUBARB

1¼ pounds rhubarb (about 3 fat stalks), topped and tailed,
then sliced crosswise into ¾-inch pieces

¼ cup superfine sugar

½ cup dry white wine, such as Sauvignon Blanc

1 vanilla bean, split lengthwise

2½ teaspoons rose water

TO SERVE THE FOOL

½ cup shelled salted roasted pistachios

Pistachio Brandy Snaps (see recipe, page 279; optional),
for scooping

Make the cardamom cream: Use the flat of your knife to smash the cardamom pods one by one. Discard the greenish husks. Pound the cardamom seeds to a powder in a mortar, then add the sugar and pound briefly.

Put the crème fraîche and heavy cream in a large mixing bowl and stir in the sugar mixture. Cover the bowl with plastic wrap and refrigerate it while you cook the rhubarb.

Make the rhubarb: Toss together the rhubarb and sugar in a bowl. Put the mixture in a medium pot and add the white wine. Use a knife to scrape the seeds from the vanilla bean into the pot; discard the pod. Set the pot over medium-low heat, bring to a very gentle simmer, and cook, tenderly stirring occasionally, until the liquid is a little creamy and the rhubarb is very tender but the pieces are still more or less intact, about 15 minutes. Set aside to cool. (To cool it quickly, scrape the mixture into another bowl, set it over a larger bowl filled with ice, and stir gently.) Once the rhubarb is completely cool, stir in the rose water.

Make the fool: Use a whisk or handheld electric mixer to whip the cream mixture until it's fluffy and full, with semi-stiff peaks. Grab four approximately 8-ounce serving containers (like rocks glasses or Ball jars) or one large bowl for a family-style presentation. It's nice if they're clear, so you can see the layers. Spoon some of the rhubarb mixture into the bottom of each glass (or into the large bowl), top with a layer of cream, and sprinkle on some pistachios. Keep layering this way until you've used everything up, making sure you finish with a layer of rhubarb.

Cover and pop into the fridge until well chilled, at least 1 hour.

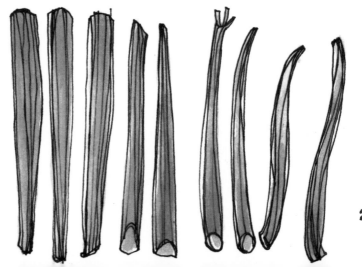

261

FENNEL-LEMON MARMALADE

I woke up one morning thinking about marmalade. The day before, a friend had brought me a little jar of his mom's marmalade, made from slightly bitter, super-sour Seville oranges. It was such a treat to have a very English snack of tea and toast with a liberal smear of marmalade that I was inspired to start experimenting, and I came up with this version. At first you can barely taste the fennel unless you know it's there, but after a day or so—the marmalade will keep in your fridge for up to a month, no processing necessary—it gets really blossomy, as if it's not made from just lemon but instead from some exotic citrus. **makes about 5 cups**

7 large firm lemons (about 2½ pounds), scrubbed well
5½ cups sugar
2 teaspoons fennel pollen

Put the lemons in a large pot and add enough water so that they'd be covered if they weren't bobbing around. Put a plate on the lemons to weigh them down. Bring the water to a boil over high heat and boil the lemons, turning them over occasionally, until you can very easily pierce their skins with a blunt knife but they're not so soft that they're bursting, about an hour. Take a look at the water now and then, just to be sure there's plenty left, and add a little more hot water if there isn't.

Cover the pot and let it sit off the heat until the lemons are cool enough to handle.

Take the lemons out of the pot, and reserve 1¼ cups of the cooking water; discard the rest. Cut the lemons crosswise in half and use a spoon to scoop the juicy pulp into a big bowl. Then break the rinds into pieces if necessary so they lie flat. Use the spoon to scrape out most of the soft pith from the rinds and discard it.

Thinly slice the rinds (about ¼ inch thick or a little thinner) and put them in the pot in which you boiled the lemons. Strain the pulp mixture through a medium-mesh sieve into the pot, smooshing it with a spoon to help it through. Discard the seeds and other fibrous bits left behind. Stir in the sugar and the reserved cooking liquid and put the pot over high heat. When it begins to simmer, tweak the heat so it simmers gently, and cook for about 1½ hours, until syrupy and orangeish. To test whether the marmalade is ready, add a spoonful to a small plate and let it cool: if it is sticky and sort of gel-like, not loose or runny, then it's ready. If not, continue simmering until it is. Stir in the fennel pollen and let the mixture cool completely.

GINGER CAKE

Every Sunday night, my dad did teatime. He laid out jam sandwiches, peanut butter on toast, and packages of Battenberg, a kind of sponge cake coated in a layer of marzipan that I always peeled off and ate first. I sort of overloaded on all those sweets—so much so that I haven't had a jam sandwich in years. But there's one sweet my dad set out that I'm still taken by: sticky, spicy ginger cake. We'd eat it with hot custard, almost invariably made from Bird's custard powder. Today I like to switch things up and serve the cake warm topped with a big dollop of cool, slightly sweetened whipped cream spiked with a little vanilla bean. My ginger cake is moist and boldly spicy from both fresh and dried ginger. It's so good that you find yourself eating it really fast. **serves 8 to 10**

1 stick (8 tablespoons) unsalted butter, at room temperature,
plus a little extra for the pan

2½ cups all-purpose flour

1 tablespoon ground ginger

1½ teaspoons ground cinnamon

¼ teaspoon ground cloves

½ teaspoon kosher salt

1 tablespoon baking powder

1½ cups boiling water

1 cup unsulfured light molasses, not blackstrap

1 teaspoon baking soda

1 packed cup dark brown sugar

1 large egg

¼ cup finely grated fresh ginger

Special Equipment
A stand or handheld electric mixer; an 8-inch
springform pan about 3 inches deep; an 8-inch
circle of parchment paper

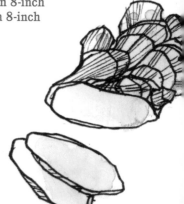

Preheat the oven to 325°F and position a rack in the middle. Grease the springform pan very well with butter. Line the bottom of the pan with the parchment paper circle and put the pan on a baking sheet.

Sift the flour, ground ginger, cinnamon, cloves, salt, and baking powder into a medium bowl and stir well. In a small pot, stir together the boiling water, molasses, and baking soda until the molasses has completely dissolved.

Put the butter and sugar in the bowl of a stand mixer fitted with the paddle attachment. (You can use a handheld electric mixer instead, if you fancy.) Mix on high speed until the mixture is light and fluffy, about 3 minutes. You'll occasionally need to scrape down the butter and sugar that clings to the sides. Reduce the mixer speed to medium-low, add the egg, and mix until incorporated. Then add the grated ginger and mix some more.

Add about one-third of the flour mixture to the butter mixture and mix on low speed until well combined. Do the same with about one-third of the molasses mixture, and repeat the process until you've used up both mixtures. Stop the mixer from time to time to scrape down the sides of the bowl. The batter will be very wet.

Pour the batter into the springform pan and place the baking sheet (pan and all) in the oven. Bake just until a cake tester inserted into the center of the cake comes out almost clean and no longer wet, about 1 hour. Before you remove the ring of the springform, let it cool a bit, though not too much—it's wonderful when it's warm.

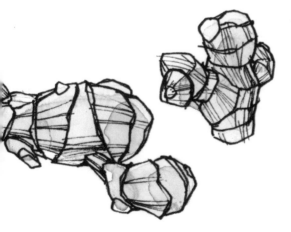

CHOCOLATE–ORANGE CAKE WITH BOURBON

Every year at Christmastime, my nan brought me a Terry's Chocolate Orange, a tinfoil-wrapped ball of orange-flavored milk chocolate that splits into segments when you knock it against a table. This is my adult version of that treat, a pudding-like, orange-zest-spiked chocolate cake with enough bourbon so that when you take a bite, you feel a gentle burn at the back of your throat.   **serves 8**

½ pound (2 sticks) unsalted butter, cut into 2-inch pieces,
plus about 1 tablespoon butter for the pan

¾ pound 70%-cacao dark chocolate, cut into medium pieces

1 cup sugar

5 large eggs

1 cup bourbon

2 teaspoons finely grated orange zest

Special Equipment
A stand mixer; a heavy 8-inch round cake pan;
an 8-inch circle of parchment paper

Put a rack in the center position of the oven. Preheat the oven to 375°F. Grease the entire inside of the cake pan very well with butter. Line the bottom of the pan with the parchment paper circle and rub butter on it, too.

Fill a medium pot with a few inches of water and bring it to a simmer over medium heat. Find a heatproof bowl that'll rest in the pot without touching the water. Put the chocolate and butter in the bowl and set the bowl on the pot. Let the chocolate and butter melt slowly, whisking now and then with a flexible silicone spatula and scraping the sides of the bowl to make sure the chocolate doesn't scorch.

Meanwhile, combine ½ cup of the sugar with the eggs in the bowl of a stand mixer fitted with the whisk attachment. Beat on medium-high until the mixture has tripled in volume, about 7 minutes.

Combine ½ cup water and the remaining ½ cup sugar in a small pan and bring to a simmer over medium heat. Cook, stirring, just until the sugar dissolves.

Warm the bourbon slightly in a small pot over low heat. Light a kitchen match,

carefully ignite the bourbon, and stand back. Wait until the flame goes out by itself. Pour the sugar-water mixture into the bourbon and add the orange zest.

Once the chocolate and butter have completely melted, whisk the bourbon mixture into the bowl. Pour the chocolate mixture into the mixer bowl with the fluffy eggs, beating on medium speed as you do. Continue beating until the chocolate and eggs are well combined, about 1 minute.

Pour the batter into the cake pan. Use both hands to carefully but firmly knock the bottom of the pan against the counter about 20 times. This forces the air out and will give the finished cake the dense, velvety texture you're after.

Line the bottom of a deep baking dish with a kitchen towel, put the cake pan in the center, and put it on the oven rack. Carefully pour enough hot water into the baking dish to come to just under the lip of the cake pan. Bake the cake just until you can cleanly pull the edge of the cake away from the sides of the pan, 30 to 40 minutes. Remove it from the oven and let it cool completely in the water bath.

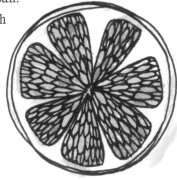

Take the cake pan out of the water and dry the sides and bottom of the pan. Invert the pan over a serving plate. Gently rap the bottom a couple of times with your palm, give the pan and plate a firm but gentle downward shake, and ease and wiggle the pan off the cake. Peel off the parchment paper and serve. Kept in a cool place, this cake can be made a few hours before you serve it.

Note: I'm not just being picky about flavor by calling for chocolate that's 70% cacao. Don't ask me why, but if it's any more or less, the cake won't set quite right in the oven.

BANOFFEE PIE

A quintessentially English treat invented by a couple of publicans at The Hungry Monk in East Sussex, this is the dessert I'd choose to end my final meal, the sweet I'd eat in my last moments on earth. A concoction that features layers of whipped cream, ripe bananas, and caramelized milk (perhaps more familiar as dulce de leche), this pie might sound too sugary. But somehow the cream cuts through all that sweetness, and when you eat it good and cold, it becomes one of those compulsively tasty desserts that you'll find yourself finishing in about ten seconds. Any cooks who dread rolling out tart dough will be thrilled to learn the grated method I suggest for this recipe and the next.

serves 12

FOR THE FILLING

Two 14-ounce cans sweetened condensed milk, labels removed

8 to 10 bananas

2 cups heavy cream

3 tablespoons confectioners' sugar

1 vanilla bean, split lengthwise

3 tablespoons finely grated bittersweet chocolate

FOR THE CRUST

1½ cups all-purpose flour

½ cup confectioners' sugar

1 stick (8 tablespoons) unsalted butter, cut into ¼-inch pieces and chilled

¼ teaspoon kosher salt

2 large egg yolks, lightly beaten

Special Equipment
A 10-inch fluted nonstick tart pan with a removable bottom; parchment paper

Note:
When you're boiling the cans of condensed milk, please make sure they're covered with water at all times. I've heard they can explode if they're not, and I'm not up for finding out!

Make the caramelized milk: Put the cans of condensed milk in a large pot and cover them generously with water. Bring the water to a boil and boil for 4 hours. Be sure the water is boiling and the cans are covered with water the entire time (this is very important)—add more boiling water to the pot if the water level threatens to get too low. Remove the cans from the pot and let them cool completely; keep them in the fridge until you're ready to use them.

Make the crust: Sift the flour into a food processor, then add the sugar, butter, and salt. Pulse until the mixture looks like fine bread crumbs. Add the yolks and pulse until a crumbly dough forms. Scrape the dough out onto a work surface and lightly knead just until smooth. Form the dough into a ball, wrap it in plastic wrap, and refrigerate it for at least 2 hours, or up to 2 days.

Preheat the oven to 350°F.

Cut the chilled dough into 2 or 3 large pieces and grate it on the large holes of a box grater. Use your fingers to press the dough onto the bottom and up the sides of the tart pan to create an even layer, the bottom about ¼ inch thick and the sides about ½ inch thick. Work swiftly—you don't want the dough to warm up too much. Gently prick the bottom here and there with a fork, then pop the pan into the freezer for 15 minutes. Cut out a 13-inch circle of parchment paper and line the dough with it. Fill the tart shell with raw rice or dried beans and set the pan on a baking sheet.

Bake the tart shell until the rim is light golden brown, 15 to 20 minutes. Remove the parchment paper and the rice or beans and bake until golden brown all over, about 15 minutes more.

Assemble the pie: Peel half of the bananas and slice them on the bias into approximately ½-inch-thick pieces. Starting from the outside and working your way to the center, arrange half of the bananas in concentric circles in the bottom of the tart shell, so each piece overlaps slightly. Gently dollop the caramelized condensed milk on top of the bananas, and spread it evenly over the slices. Cover with plastic wrap and put it in the fridge to chill, up to 2 hours.

While the pie is chilling, combine the cream and the confectioners' sugar in a bowl. Use a knife to scrape the vanilla bean seeds into the cream; discard the pod. Use a whisk or a handheld electric mixer to whip the cream to soft peaks. Cover it, too, and chill in the fridge.

Peel and slice the remaining bananas. Add another layer of bananas. Give the whipped cream a good, brief whisk, then spread it over the pie so it completely covers the bananas. Sprinkle the grated chocolate over the top.

Serve straightaway, when it's still good and cold.

tea

I take my tea strong. Always English Breakfast, PG Tips brand, with a little milk. No sugar—at least, not anymore. I'll let it sit there until it cools enough that I can chug it back, but it's still hot enough to just barely scorch the back of my throat. I like how drinking hot tea in the kitchen makes me sweat a bit, which cools me down. I like the way the caffeine creeps up on you, how it gradually wakes you up.

And I like biscuits with my tea, for dipping. I have a thing for them, especially any with a filling—custard cream, Tim Tams, Oreos. I also like oatmeal raisin and ginger. I can finish a whole pack in ten minutes.

For a perfect cuppa, bring a kettle of water to a boil. Put a bag of PG Tips English Breakfast tea in an 8-ounce mug (not a wide mug, please, or the tea will cool too quickly) and pour in the boiling water. Let the bag steep until the tea is good and strong, then toss the bag. Stir in about a tablespoon of whole milk. Drink it with a pack of biscuits or a plate of Soft Oatmeal Cookies (see recipe, page 277) alongside.

PINE NUT TART

This is my take on treacle tart, a dessert favorite of many an English child, and which I loved as a kid. It's not unlike Pennsylvania Dutch shoofly pie. Both share a sticky-sweet filling made from the leavings of sugar-making—molasses in the case of shoofly, golden syrup in the case of treacle tart. Here the golden syrup is mixed with lemon zest, sherry, and toasty pine nuts.   **serves 6 to 8**

FOR THE CRUST

1½ cups all-purpose flour

½ cup confectioners' sugar

1 stick (8 tablespoons) unsalted butter, chilled
and cut into ¼-inch pieces

¼ teaspoon kosher salt

2 large egg yolks, lightly beaten

FOR THE FILLING

½ cup pine nuts

2 large eggs, lightly beaten

¼ cup coarse bread crumbs (see Bread Crumbs, page 12)

One 454-gram can Lyle's Golden Syrup
(see Golden Syrup, page 275)

2 tablespoons heavy cream

Finely grated zest of 4 large lemons

¼ cup fino sherry

½ teaspoon Maldon or another flaky sea salt

Special Equipment
A 9-inch fluted nonstick tart pan
with a removable bottom; parchment paper

Make the crust: Sift the flour into a food processor, then add the sugar, butter, and salt. Pulse until the mixture looks like fine bread crumbs. Add the yolks and pulse until a crumbly dough forms. Scrape the dough out onto a work surface and lightly knead just until smooth. Form the dough into a ball, wrap it in plastic wrap, and refrigerate it for at least an hour, or up to 2 days.

Preheat the oven to 350°F.

Cut the chilled dough into 2 or 3 large pieces and grate it on the large holes of a box grater. Use your fingers to press the dough onto the bottom and up the sides of the tart pan to create an even layer, the bottom about ¼ inch thick and the sides about ½ inch thick. Work swiftly—you don't want the dough to warm up too much. Gently prick the bottom here and there with a fork, which will prevent it from puffing up as it bakes, then pop the pan into the freezer for 15 minutes. Cut out a 12-inch circle of parchment paper and line the dough with it. Fill the tart shell with raw rice or dried beans.

Put the tart on a baking sheet and bake the tart shell just until the rim is light golden brown, 15 to 25 minutes. Carefully remove the parchment paper and rice or beans. (You can save the rice or beans to use the next time you bake.)

Meanwhile, make the filling: Heat a small pan over medium heat. Add the pine nuts and toast them, shaking the pan and tossing the nuts frequently, until they go shiny and evenly golden brown, about 4 minutes. Transfer them to a medium mixing bowl.

Once the pine nuts are cool, add the remaining filling ingredients, and whisk until really well combined.

Right before you add the filling to the tart shell, give it a good stir, then slowly pour it into the shell. Bake the tart until the filling is just set but the center still jiggles slightly when you give the pan a gentle shake, 25 to 35 minutes. Let cool slightly before slicing.

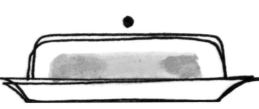

GOLDEN SYRUP

Golden syrup is a thick, pale-amber-colored form of sugar syrup, made in the process of refining sugarcane juice into sugar. It's used in a lot of traditional English desserts—it is the main ingredient in steamed treacle pudding—and Lyle's is one of the oldest brands around. Their golden syrup comes in a charming tin emblazoned with a lion that you can reuse once the syrup's gone. There's no real substitute for golden syrup, but if you can't lay hands on any, you can substitute two parts light corn syrup and one part molasses.

SOFT OATMEAL COOKIES

As I said, I could down a whole pack of biscuits in one go. And as much as I adore Tim Tams and Oreos and gingerbread, I often find myself reaching for these soft oatmeal cookies studded with sweet-tart raisins and winey currants. I suppose you could bake them longer, until they go crunchy, but I like mine this way. A soft cookie makes me go back for just one more bite (as you say to yourself again and again), just one more bite.

makes 16 cookies

¼ cup golden raisins

¼ cup dark sultanas or golden raisins

¼ cup dried currants

1¼ sticks (10 tablespoons) unsalted butter,
at room temperature

1 cup packed light brown sugar

2 large eggs

1 cup all-purpose flour

½ teaspoon baking soda

½ teaspoon ground cinnamon

Large pinch of kosher salt

2 teaspoons vanilla extract

2 cups rolled oats

Special Equipment
A stand or handheld electric mixer;
parchment paper

Combine the raisins, sultanas, and currants in a bowl, add enough water to over, and let them soak in the fridge for at least 5 hours or overnight. Drain and discard the water.

Preheat the oven to 350°F. Line a large cookie sheet or baking sheet with parchment paper.

Put the butter and sugar in the bowl of a stand mixer fitted with the paddle attachment. (You can use a handheld electric mixer instead, if you fancy.) Mix on high speed until the mixture is light and fluffy, about 4 minutes. You'll occasionally need to scrape down the butter and sugar that clings to the sides. Crack in one egg and beat for 30 seconds, then add the other egg and beat for 30 seconds more.

Sift the flour, baking soda, cinnamon, and salt into a medium bowl and stir well. Add to the egg mixture, along with the vanilla extract, scrape down the sides of the bowl, and mix at medium speed just until the ingredients are well mixed and the flour is evenly distributed. Add the oats, raisins, sultanas, and currants and mix just until they're evenly distributed. Cover the bowl with plastic wrap and pop it in the fridge to chill, at least an hour.

Use your hands to divide the dough into 16 equal balls (about 2½ tablespoons each) and place half on the lined sheet, leaving about 2 inches between them. Bake for about 20 minutes, rotating the pan after about 10 minutes, just until they go golden brown all over and firm at the edges and no longer feel sticky or gooey when you touch one with your finger. Let the cookies cool on a rack as you bake the second batch.

Eat the cookies slightly warm, when they're cakey, or when they've cooled completely.

PISTACHIO BRANDY SNAPS

These thin, crispy tuile-like treats make a fine partner for slightly milky tea. But they're even better used as edible spoons—in England, they're often molded into cannoli-like tubes—for scooping up the tart and creamy layers of Rhubarb Fool (see recipe, page 260). **makes about 40**

½ cup sugar

1 stick (8 tablespoons) unsalted butter

⅓ cup Lyle's golden syrup (see Golden Syrup, page 275)

1 teaspoon finely grated orange zest

¼ teaspoon ground ginger

¼ teaspoon ground cinnamon

½ teaspoon kosher salt

⅓ cup all-purpose flour

¼ cup finely chopped salted roasted pistachios

2 tablespoons brandy

Special Equipment
A nonstick baking mat, such as a Silpat, or parchment paper

Combine the sugar, butter, golden syrup, orange zest, spices, and salt in a small pot and bring to a boil over medium-high heat, then immediately remove from the heat. Whisk in the flour and pistachios. Stir in the brandy. The batter will be as thick as peanut butter. Let it cool.

Put a rack in the center position of the oven. Preheat the oven to 350°F. Line a baking sheet with a nonstick baking mat or parchment paper. You'll need to bake the cookies in several batches.

Spoon on ½ tablespoon of the batter for each cookie, leaving a couple of inches between them, as the batter will spread quite a bit in baking; you should have 6 cookies on the sheet. Bake until the brandy snaps are deep golden brown, about 12 minutes. Let them cool slightly, then slide a thin spatula around and under the perimeter of each snap to loosen it. Let them cool completely and serve.

dressings, sauces, and condiments

lemon caper

salsa verde

pesto

mayonnaise

aioli

romesco

horseradish
sauce

tarragon

chimichurri

LEMON CAPER DRESSING

This is one of the first recipes I ever came up with myself, back when I worked at The Brackenbury in West London. What I liked about it then and still do today is that each bite delivers little explosions of flavor—salty hits of caper, tart blasts of lemon, sharp little hits of mustard, and an edge of shallot, all rounded out by an almost undetectable pinch of sugar. Finely chopped parsley is a welcome addition. I love to serve it with fatty foods, like Fried Pig's Ear Salad (see recipe, page 86).   **makes about 1 cup**

2 medium lemons
3 tablespoons finely chopped shallots
2 tablespoons Dijon mustard
2 tablespoons drained capers, finely chopped
½ teaspoon Maldon or another flaky sea salt
½ teaspoon superfine sugar
¼ cup extra virgin olive oil

Segment the lemons (see Segmenting Lemons, below). Squeeze the juice from the membranes into a separate bowl, add the rest of the ingredients, and stir well. Add the lemon segments and toss gently to coat them without breaking them up. Use straightaway or chill in the fridge, covered, for up to an hour.

SEGMENTING LEMONS

Yes, you are up for segmenting lemons, if that's what you're fretting about. It's quite easy to separate the glossy little wedges of lemon flesh from the fruit's membranes. And they're such a pleasure to eat, without any of the chewy, stringy bits. Even though I've been cooking for a long time, I still take pride in my segments, in carving away the skin and pith from the fruit carefully so that when I'm done, the lemon still looks like a lemon, not a ragged hexagonal thing, then cutting out each wedge. The Roux brothers, the first French chefs in England to get a Michelin star, tested cooks looking for a job by making them fry an egg. Maybe I'll start making cooks segment a lemon.

So here's how to do it: Use a sharp knife to cut off just enough of the fruit's top and bottom to

LEMON—OLIVE OIL DRESSING

The success of this dressing, which we used often at The River Café, is in its proportions. It's the simplest combination of ingredients imaginable, and it tastes great because they're all in just the right balance. You can taste the bright acidity of the lemon, you can taste the grassiness of the olive oil. It's seasoned with just enough salt. When you shake them all together, they get creamy and emulsified. You'll find yourself using this dressing on salads, of course, but also to add brightness to everything from grilled fish to boiled potatoes. Make it right before you plan to use it.

makes about 1¼ cups

½ cup freshly squeezed lemon juice, or to taste

1 cup extra virgin olive oil, or to taste

1½ teaspoons Maldon or another flaky sea salt,
crushed between your fingers

Freshly ground black pepper (optional)

Put the lemon juice, oil, salt, and, if you fancy, pepper in a squeeze bottle or a plastic container with a lid. Shake really well, taste, and add a little more lemon or olive oil, if you like (some lemons are more acidic than others). Set it aside until you're ready to use it, and shake again just before you do.

Note:
This recipe can be easily halved, quartered, or doubled.

expose a full circle of the flesh on either end. Stand the lemon on one of its ends, place your knife point at the seam where the fruit meets the pith, and use a gentle sawing motion to cut away a wide strip of pith and skin, following the curve of the fruit from top to bottom. The first cut is the hardest to get right. You'll get better with each one. Repeat the process until all you have left is a nice, round, naked fruit—just lemon segments separated by translucent walls of membrane. If you've missed any white pith, trim it off. Put the lemon on its side, make a cut down either side of a segment, right against the membrane, and gently pry out the segment. Repeat to remove the remaining segments. Flick out any seeds, and set the segments aside in a bowl, reserving the juicy membranes.

the river café

I'd been cooking at good restaurants for ten years before I got a job at The River Café. I used to watch the owners, Rose Gray and Ruth Rogers, on TV. I loved how Rose threw salt casually but deliberately into pasta water. I loved how they kept their food rustic and never chopped anything too fine. Once I saw them boil *cavolo nero* (black kale), then puree it with some garlic and good Tuscan olive oil, the kind that smells like freshly cut grass. They tossed the mixture with pasta, and I thought, I have to make that!

I got lucky—I knew someone who worked at The River Café, so I called him up and worked out a time to come and trail in the kitchen for two weeks—a sort of job audition. When I turned up, I was really nervous and must have seemed it. Rose took a peek at me and gave me this look of death. I scuttled off to prep. During my trail, Rose told me to finely chop onions, so I got to it, painstakingly transforming them with my knife into tiny dice, as I had been taught in cooking school and by chefs in other restaurants. But when Rose and Ruth saw what I'd been doing, they stopped me. Not *that* fine, they said, amused at this young cook. I was thrilled. I realized right then that this was a different kind of cooking. It wasn't rigid. It was natural, almost instinctual, yet no less passionate for it. Plus, chopping anything that fine is a pain in the backside.

One day early on, I was tasked with making a pasta sauce with fresh walnuts from Rose and Ruth's cookbook. I boiled the walnuts in milk to get the skins off, following the recipe's instructions. The walnuts were really fiddly, so I ended up peeling them with my fingertips and got the skins under my nails. (After work that day, I went to my second job and my thumbs were throbbing so much I had to dunk them in cold water to make them stop. But the pain felt good. It was proof that I'd been working hard.) I pounded the walnuts with garlic and herbs in a mortar, mixed in milk-soaked bread, tossed the sauce with pasta, and tasted it. It was like being hit on the head with a cast-iron pan. I knew then that this was the kind of food I wanted to cook: rustic food elevated by careful preparation. As elegant as the dishes were, you always had the feeling that an Italian grandmother might have made them.

ROQUEFORT DRESSING

This dressing is meant for Escarole Salad with Roquefort, Pears, and Walnuts (see recipe, page 92), but it also makes a fine dip for raw and blanched vegetables.

makes 1½ cups

5 ounces Roquefort
¼ cup crème fraîche
¼ cup heavy cream
¼ cup extra virgin olive oil
1½ teaspoons Maldon or another flaky sea salt
5 tablespoons champagne vinegar
¼ teaspoon finely grated garlic (about 1 medium clove)

Crumble the Roquefort into a medium bowl, and add the crème fraîche, cream, olive oil, salt, vinegar, and garlic. Give it all a good stir so the dressing goes creamy and everything's well mixed but there are still chunks of Roquefort to provide bursts of saltiness. Use right away, or cover the bowl with plastic wrap and pop it into the fridge to chill.

GREEN GODDESS

A few years back, the food writer Amanda Hesser wrote an article for the *New York Times Magazine* on green goddess dressing, a sort of herby, vinegary, anchovy-spiked mayonnaise-based concoction. She called me to see if I'd dream up a modern edition—the article was for the magazine's "Recipe Redux" column, in which chefs reimagine old *Times* recipes. I deconstructed a straight green goddess dressing and served it as a condiment with lamb. But the classic—which I had heard of but never tasted—really got my attention. My riff on this '50s California dressing includes avocado but no anchovy. The thick, rich result is more like an herbaceous mayonnaise, and I love it as a dip for vegetables. Add more garlic and it would make a quirky stand-in for aioli. Try it with Stewed Octopus with Butter Beans (see recipe, page 107), or as layers in Chilled Crab Trifle (see recipe, page 99). Loosen it with a touch of water (then reseason it), and it makes a great dressing for sturdy lettuces like Bibb, Romaine, and Little Gem. **makes about 2 cups**

1 medium Hass avocado

¼ cup finely chopped chives

¼ cup finely chopped tarragon leaves

1 medium garlic clove, finely chopped

½ cup heavy cream

1 large egg yolk

1 tablespoon freshly squeezed lemon juice, or to taste

1 teaspoon Maldon or another flaky sea salt

½ cup extra virgin olive oil

Halve and pit the avocado, then scoop the flesh into a blender. Add the rest of the ingredients except for the oil and blend, stopping to prod and stir to help them blend, until the mixture is very smooth. Then, with the motor running, drizzle in the olive oil in a nice steady stream, stirring occasionally if necessary, until it's all well combined.

Pour the dressing into a bowl. Have a taste and add more salt and/or lemon juice, if you fancy. Use it right away.

SALSA VERDE

You can really taste each herb in this fresh, vinegary condiment: you get the vibrant parsley first, then a few seconds later you taste the slightly astringent mint, and finally it culminates in the musty, earthy marjoram. Underneath all that is the umami from the anchovies and capers. The key to making it is to use your sharpest chef's knife to chop the herbs and to chop with urgency. That way, the herbs will transform into a lovely loose paste, not a muddy mush.   **makes about 1 cup**

3 whole salt-packed anchovies, rinsed, soaked, and filleted
(see Filleting Salt-Packed Anchovies, page 10)

1 heaping tablespoon drained capers

½ small garlic clove, smashed and peeled

1 tablespoon Dijon mustard

¼ cup plus 2 tablespoons extra virgin olive oil

3 tablespoons red wine vinegar

A giant handful of small, delicate flat-leaf parsley sprigs
(about 4 lightly packed cups, if you insist)

A large handful of mint leaves (about half as much as the parsley)

A handful of marjoram leaves (about half as much as the mint)

Maldon or another flaky sea salt

Freshly ground black pepper (optional)

Put the anchovy fillets on your cutting board along with the capers and garlic and chop them all to a fine paste. Be patient, chopping, gathering it all together, and then chopping again until you can't tell the anchovy from the caper and you can barely make out the garlic. It might take you several minutes, depending on your speed. Scrape the paste into a mixing bowl.

Add the mustard, olive oil, and vinegar to the bowl and stir really well. (You could stop right here and you'd have a great sauce.)

Toss all the herbs together on the cutting board—this way, the mint and marjoram won't discolor so quickly. Bunch the pile together with your hands and slice the leaves as fine as you can, then go at it, chopping with vigor and tossing and chopping until it's all finely chopped.

Add the herbs to the bowl and stir really well. It should be ready to go, but have a taste and add a little salt and a few turns of pepper, if you'd like.

TARRAGON SAUCE

This sauce is similar to the one that Rose and Ruth served at The River Café as a condiment for *bollito misto*. The sauce brightens and cuts through the richness of my *bollito misto*–inspired Tongue Sandwiches (see recipe, page 141), so you're always ready to take yet another bite. It would be equally fine with roast beef on a crusty roll. **makes a generous 1 cup**

¼ cup rustic bread torn into small crustless pieces
3½ tablespoons red wine vinegar
2 tablespoons drained capers, finely chopped
4 whole salted-packed anchovies, rinsed, soaked, and filleted
(see Filleting Salt-Packed Anchovies, page 10), then finely chopped
⅛ teaspoon finely chopped garlic
1 tablespoon Dijon mustard
¼ cup olive oil
A large handful of tarragon leaves
1 hard-boiled egg
Freshly ground black pepper
Maldon or another flaky sea salt

Put the bread in a medium mixing bowl, pour in the vinegar, and let the mixture sit for 2 minutes. Break up the bread with your fingertips.

Mix the capers, anchovies, and garlic on your cutting board and chop them together until the mixture is slightly creamy looking and almost paste-like. Scoop it up with your knife and pop it into the bowl of vinegar-soaked bread, then stir in the mustard and olive oil.

Gently gather the tarragon leaves into a little ball and use a sharp knife to finely chop them. Add it all to the bowl.

Separate the white of the hard-boiled egg from its yolk. Finely crumble the yolk and chop the white, then add them to the bowl. Stir well and have a taste. Add a little pepper and salt to taste.

BASIL OR SAGE PESTO

One method, two types of pesto. Both are so simple to make—I don't even toast the pine nuts. I like to leave pesto a little chunky, but you can make it as smooth as you like. The classic basil version is especially lovely in the spring, perhaps dolloped onto Gnudi (see recipe, page 231) or Swiss Chard wih Olive Oil (see recipe, page 220). The sage version tastes of autumn, intensely sagey and salty, so just a few spoonfuls can deliver a real wallop of flavor. It's just the thing for Roasted Veg (see recipe, page 208).

Make either one right before you plan to eat it, because it will quickly turn brown on you. To help prevent this, scrape the pesto into a bowl and either cover with plastic wrap, pressing it against the surface, or drizzle on just enough olive oil to make a thin layer that completely covers the pesto. **makes about 1 cup**

2 giant handfuls of basil leaves or 2 small handfuls of sage leaves

½ medium garlic clove, roughly chopped

3 tablespoons pine nuts

A 1-ounce chunk of Parmesan, finely grated

1 teaspoon Maldon or another flaky sea salt

About ½ cup extra virgin olive oil

Put the basil or sage in a small food processor and add the garlic, pine nuts, cheese, and salt. Pulse a few times, then add most of the oil (you may use a little less or a little more than ½ cup, depending on how big your herb handfuls are), then process full-on, scraping down the sides of the processor or stirring gently if need be, until the mixture is well combined but still chunky. Taste and season with more salt, if you fancy.

CHIMICHURRI

As Wikipedia legend has it, chimichurri was named for an Irish soldier called Jimmy McCurry, who first made it and whose name Argentineans badly mispronounced. My version of this vibrant Argentinean sauce, which brightens up pretty much anything, is quite shalloty, with a little minced habanero swimming around in there looking sexy, and a couple of handfuls of herbs chopped really fine (a good, sharp knife is essential). I call for mint, so it goes great with lamb, but you could substitute the traditional oregano, or chervil, or maybe heartier herbs like thyme and rosemary during wintertime. Maybe you'd like it chunkier, more lemony, or less spicy than I do. Chimichurri is a classic accompaniment to a beautiful steak and, oh, it's so good when it mixes with the meaty juices . . . but wouldn't it also be nice with some grilled beef tongue or hearts? **makes about 1 cup**

⅓ cup tightly packed very finely chopped shallots
(about 2 medium shallots)
½ teaspoon very finely chopped garlic (about 1 medium clove)
⅔ cup extra virgin olive oil
A big handful of small, delicate flat-leaf parsley sprigs
A big handful of mint leaves
1 teaspoon seeded and finely chopped habanero chili
A generous pinch of Maldon or another flaky sea salt
2 tablespoons freshly squeezed lemon juice, or to taste

Combine the shallots, garlic, and olive oil in a bowl.

Toss the herbs together on a cutting board (this will keep your mint from going brown on you) and chop them very fine. Add the herbs and habanero to the bowl and stir the mixture really well. Add the salt, then let the sauce sit for a few minutes or up to 2 hours while the herbs get to know each other. Right before you are ready to serve it, stir in the lemon juice. Taste the chimichurri, season it again with salt and/or lemon juice if you need to, and serve.

ROMESCO SAUCE

Smoky, tart, and a little sweet, romesco is a burnt-sienna blend of cooked vegetables flecked with red and green chunks of tomato and pepper and little black bits of char. It's just as thrilling to eat as it is to look at, and I reckon you'll find it as tasty with fish and meat as you do with vegetables straight from the steamer or grill. You might even want to do as they do in Catalonia, Spain: Char spring onions over an open fire, then wrap them in newspaper and let them steam until they're tender. Once they're sufficiently tender, you grab one, peel off the blackish outer layer, and dunk the bulb into romesco. Lovely.

  This recipe makes a big batch, but you'll be happy to have more than you think you need—and it keeps well.   **makes about 2 cups**

About 1 pound ripe medium tomatoes, blanched, peeled, and cored
(see Tomatoes, page 10)

1 medium red bell pepper

1 small poblano pepper

1 small purple bell pepper (or another poblano)

6 similarly sized cipollini onions (a little less than ½ pound),
or a small red onion cut into 8 wedges

7 medium garlic cloves, peeled

½ cup unsalted skinless Marcona almonds

½ cup fine bread crumbs (see Bread Crumbs, page 12)

½ cup plus 1 tablespoon extra virgin olive oil

3 tablespoons sherry vinegar, or to taste

1½ teaspoons hot *pimentón* (Spanish smoked paprika)

3 tablespoons Maldon or another flaky sea salt

Heat a large griddle or grill pan over medium-high heat until it just begins to smoke. Cook the tomatoes, peppers, onions, garlic, and almonds on the hot surface (in batches, if necessary) and turn them occasionally to make sure they cook evenly: cook the almonds and garlic until lightly charred, about 5 minutes; cook the tomatoes, small peppers, and onions until charred in spots, 10 to 15 minutes; and cook the peppers until they are blistered all over, charred in spots, and soft but not collapsed, about 20 minutes. As they finish cooking, transfer the vegetables to a big bowl and the almonds to the food processor.

Process the almonds until they are a mixture of fine and chunky bits. Pour them into a large mixing bowl.

Remove the peppers' stems. Cut the peppers lengthwise in half, wipe out the seeds, and trim off the pale ribs. Scrape off the skin with a knife or pull it off with your fingers. Whatever you do, don't run the peppers under water.

Roughly chop the vegetables, then put them in the food processor and blend until the mixture is fairly smooth but with plenty of small chunks here and there. Add the vegetables to the bowl with the almonds and stir in the bread crumbs, olive oil, vinegar, *pimentón*, and salt. Have a taste and add more salt and/or vinegar, if you'd like.

Covered with plastic wrap, the sauce will keep in the fridge for up to 5 days.

HORSERADISH SAUCE

This is a bright and lovely sauce that takes no time to make. I fancy the tingle you get from the horseradish and the brightness the lemon brings. A cool spoonful in hot soup or on roast beef is perfect, and I especially like it dolloped around Cabbage and Bacon (see recipe, page 172) or in place of the simple grated horseradish on Tongue Sandwiches (see recipe, page 141). **makes about 1 cup**

¼ pound fresh horseradish, peeled and finely grated

½ cup crème fraîche

2 tablespoons extra virgin olive oil

¾ teaspoon kosher salt

½ lemon

Combine the horseradish, crème fraîche, olive oil, salt, and a good squeeze of lemon juice in a small bowl. Stir it together well, using a gentle hand so the sauce doesn't separate. Use it right away, or cover the bowl with plastic wrap and chill until you're ready for it, as long as 24 hours.

Note: It's good if you tear up while you're grating the horseradish. If you do, it means the root is plenty pungent and will provide the nose-tickling sting you're after. If you don't, you might want to go to the store and buy another root.

AIOLI

In the late '90s, I worked at The Brackenbury in Hammersmith. The chef there, Adam Robinson, feisty and a bit camp, wore espadrilles, pants rolled up to his calves, and square-rimmed glasses. He was an innovator of gastropub food, though I'm not sure he thought about it like that. He just made simple food, but did it so well. One of the loveliest dishes at The Brackenbury was a grand platter of boiled duck eggs and all manner of veg, and at the center of it all was a pot of aioli, the fantastic velvety, garlicky olive oil–based mayonnaise. At the first incarnation of The John Dory, in homage to Adam, I served aioli alongside soft-shell crab, roasted beets, deep-fried artichokes, and confited garlic. As you can see, the luscious stuff goes well with so much—Grilled Sea Bass (see recipe, page 115), seafood stews like Stewed Octopus with Butter Beans (see recipe, page 107), Seafood Salad (see recipe, page 111), or anything Mediterranean, really, whether it's stirred into a soup or slathered on lamb.   **makes 1¾ cups**

1 medium-large garlic clove, halved lengthwise
1 teaspoon Maldon or another flaky sea salt
5 teaspoons freshly squeezed lemon juice
2 large egg yolks, at room temperature
1½ cups extra virgin olive oil

Note:
To make saffron aioli, stir ⅛ teaspoon saffron threads into the lemon juice, let the mixture sit for a few minutes, then follow the recipe.

Put the garlic and salt in a mortar and pound until you have a smooth paste. (You can also mince the garlic on a chopping board, add the salt, and make a paste with a knife or fork.) Transfer the paste to a bowl, add the lemon juice, and stir until well combined. Add the egg yolks and whisk vigorously until the yolks go pale and the mixture is frothy, about 1 minute. Steady the bowl by wrapping a damp kitchen towel around the base. Slowly, *slowly*, drizzle in a nice steady stream of olive oil, whisking with a sense of urgency the whole time, until you've added about half of it. Whisk in 1 teaspoon water, then slowly drizzle in the rest of the oil, whisking as before—keep whisking until the oil is really well combined and the aioli is thick and velvety. Whisk in another pinch of salt and/or a little more lemon juice, if you'd like. It keeps in the fridge for up to 3 days.

MAYONNAISE

I always frown at people who tell me they don't like mayonnaise. Sure, the store-bought stuff leaves a lot to be desired, but homemade mayo is the most amazing thing. Everyone should know how easy it is to make at home, how the magic of emulsification turns simple oil, vinegar, and egg yolks into a light and incredibly silky condiment. Just thinking about it makes me want a tuna sandwich—a creamy blend of tuna, celery leaf, fennel fronds, and lemon, with maybe a bit of chopped celery for crunch. Or bread slathered with parsley-flecked mayo, draped with boiled ham, and topped with tender pea shoots. The mayo is never quite the main event, but it certainly helps everything else along.   **makes about 1½ cups**

4 large egg yolks, at room temperature
2 teaspoons Dijon mustard
2 tablespoons champagne vinegar
½ teaspoon Maldon or another flaky sea salt
Slightly more than 1 cup peanut or sunflower oil

Combine the egg yolks, mustard, vinegar, and salt in a bowl and whisk vigorously until the yolks go pale and the mixture is frothy, about 1 minute. Slowly, *slowly*, drizzle in a nice steady stream of the oil, whisking with a sense of urgency the whole time, until you've added all of it—keep whisking until the oil is really well combined and the mayo is silky smooth and a pale, barely-there yellow from the egg yolks. It keeps in the fridge for up to 3 days.

MAKING AIOLI AND MAYONNAISE IN THE FOOD PROCESSOR

FOR AIOLI: Crush the garlic and salt to a paste in a mortar. Scrape the paste into a small food processor, add the egg yolks, and process until well combined. Add the lemon juice and process again until well combined. Process the whole time as you pour in half of the oil in a steady stream. Then add 1 teaspoon of water, process, and add the remaining oil in a steady stream, processing the whole time. If the aioli splits (that is, if it has a curdy rather than a completely smooth texture), add another teaspoon of water and process for 10 seconds or so.

FOR MAYONNAISE: Combine the egg yolks, mustard, vinegar, and salt in a small food processor and process until pale, about 30 seconds. Slowly pour in the oil in a steady stream, processing the whole time, until the mayonnaise is thick and creamy.

a couple stocks

cooking school

When I found out I'd sent in my police officer application too late and would have to wait two years to reapply, I decided I had to do something worthwhile in the meantime. My two older sisters were in cooking school, so I decided to give it a go. The first step was an entrance exam. It worried me, but somehow I passed, even though in my interview, I admitted that I was rubbish at math and percentages. Still am.

The school had a focus on the culinary arts, but it also offered classes in hotel management and hairdressing. As you can imagine, I avoided those. I learned the fundamentals—how to make stocks and sauces, how to butcher— and picked up bits of wisdom along the way. I remember a teacher demonstrating how to dismantle a chicken. I asked, "But how will I know how to break down the next chicken?" Well, he said, the bones are always going to be in the same place. Remember, I was just sixteen at the time, so this was particularly profound.

While I was in cooking school, I also had to work to earn money—I knew I didn't want to stay in Birmingham. My goal was to move to London, where my sister was living and working, so I set out to save up enough for a bedsit—sort of like what Americans call a studio, but not as glamorous and so named because the only place to sit is the bed. My school assigned me to work at Boots, a department store, and I was hoping to cook at the café. But for some reason, they stuck me in the photo department, working the till. It was a disaster, mainly because I was shit at math. One summer, I worked as a chambermaid, pushing around a little trolley, changing beds, and dusting hotel rooms.

Finally I got a gig cooking. Nowadays an ambitious student in cooking school might aim to put in some hours at her city's best restaurants. I took a job at the Holiday Inn. I worked a bit of room service, a bit of the veg station, and a bit on carvery, slicing and plating roasts. It wasn't glamorous, but it was fun to work in such a big, busy place. On my last day, as a sort of prize, my boss told me I could cook a dish that would be served that night. I just about shat myself. I decided to cook something I'd cooked for a school exam—chicken Veronique, an old-school fricassee with cream, tarragon, and grapes. I think it sold pretty well.

STICKY CHICKEN STOCK

There's almost always a big vat of stock simmering away on the stove at my restaurants, bones and veg spending quality time together, bestowing their rich flavor to gently bubbling water. The collagen in a pig's foot makes it a rich, porky, and sticky addition to basic chicken stocks. This stock lends a luscious viscosity to stews and sauces and dishes like Faggots (see recipe, page 199) and Cabbage and Bacon (see recipe, page 172). When it cools, it sets to a jiggly solid—it's perfect for making anything set in jelly or terrines. I love the sound the semisolidified stock makes as you scoop it out, a satisfying, suction-induced *thoop* that hints at the richness to come.

makes about 3 quarts

5 pounds chicken bones, such as backs, wings, and necks,
cut into big chunks by your butcher

3 pounds pig trotters, split lengthwise by your butcher

1 large Spanish onion, quartered

1 medium carrot, peeled and halved lengthwise

3 celery stalks, halved crosswise

2 heads garlic, halved horizontally

20 black peppercorns

2 fresh bay leaves, or 1 dried

1 thyme sprig

Note:

For a more classic chicken stock, omit the pig trotters and use 6 quarts of water instead of 4. I suggest making a big batch of this to have on hand whether you're cooking Seven-Vegetable Soup (see recipe, page 62) or any old thing, really. This makes about 5 quarts.

Combine all the ingredients in a large pot, add 4 quarts water, and bring it to a simmer over medium-high heat. Lower the heat to maintain a very gentle simmer and cook, keeping an eye on it, until the pig's feet start to fall apart, 5 to 6 hours. You can walk away from the stove, have a tea, and flip through some cookbooks while you do this, but do check on it now and then, skimming the gunk off the surface and tweaking the heat, if necessary—if it boils, or if you stir it, you'll end up with a cloudy stock.

Fish out and discard the bones, trotters, and vegetables. Strain the liquid through a fine-mesh sieve into a large bowl and toss out the solids. Let it cool completely. It will be like jelly. Scrape off the white fat and store the stock in the fridge for up to 3 days, or in the freezer for up to a month.

FISH STOCK

This quick and simple stock provides the backbone for Smoked Haddock Chowder (see recipe, page 68). You'll need only 2 cups of it for that, but I suggest making a big batch and freezing the rest, because it's great to have on hand. You can buy bones from your fishmonger (ask for those from white-fleshed fish that aren't too oily, such as bass, fluke, cod, halibut, and sole). Or save bones from your cooking endeavors, popping them into a big bag that you store in your freezer and add to as the weeks pass.   **makes about 3 quarts**

5 pounds fish bones
½ small Spanish onion, quartered
5 skin-on garlic cloves
1 small celery stalk, chopped into thirds
A small handful of fennel fronds (optional)
A small handful of flat-leaf parsley stems (optional)

If the bones have the heads attached, discard the eyes and use scissors to remove the gills. Rinse the bones well under running water, rubbing off any blood with your fingers. All this stuff can make your stock a bit bitter, so it's good to get rid of it.

Chop the bones, if necessary, so they fit comfortably in a large pot. Combine the bones and the remaining ingredients in the pot with just enough cold water to almost, but not completely, cover the bones, about 3½ quarts. Bring the water to a simmer over high heat (do not let it boil, or you'll end up with cloudy stock), then immediately lower the heat and cook at a very gentle simmer until the flavor has an essence of the ocean, about 30 minutes.

Set a fine-mesh sieve over a large bowl and ladle in the stock; discard the solids. Store it in the fridge for up to 3 days, or in the freezer for up to a month.

libations

A BLOODY MARY

My favorite bar in San Francisco is a place called Zeitgeist. It's a bike-messenger hang-out with a huge beer garden, a nice burger, and the Tamale Lady, who goes around sell-ing tamales. It has this really nice vibe. During the months I was working at Chez Panisse I'd go to Zeitgeist on my free afternoons, have a chat with friends, and get a little buzz from an icy Bloody Mary (or three) and the little glass of beer that came alongside. This recipe is my ode to those afternoons, a simple drink for a party or brunch.

Before you start mixing, let me say that this is how I like my Bloody Mary. Everyone has a different take on which ingredients they think should stand out. So, as you add this and that, keep your goal in mind. My favorites are the horseradish and celery—the celery salt throughout and the now-and-then pleasure of coming across a celery leaf. Still, I want to be able to sense each component, and not even the star ingredients should overpower the others. After you add the alcohol, the flavor will change as the vodka amplifies the horseradish and black pepper. Use the best tomato juice you can find, one that tastes like fresh tomatoes and is not overly salty or artificially sweet. **makes 4 drinks**

A 2-ounce piece fresh horseradish

4 cups bottled tomato juice

¼ cup Worcestershire sauce

½ teaspoon freshly ground black pepper

½ teaspoon celery salt

1 heaping teaspoon finely grated lemon zest

1 tablespoon freshly squeezed lemon juice

4 teaspoons Tapatio hot sauce, or your favorite brand

A small handful of chopped celery leaves

8 ounces vodka

Ice cubes

Peel the horseradish, finely grate it, and measure out a packed ⅓ cup. Stir together the horseradish and all the remaining ingredients except the vodka and ice in a large pitcher. Have a taste and add a little more of this or that, if you'd like. Stir in the vodka, then taste and tweak again.

Fill four large glasses halfway with ice and pour in the Bloody Marys. Con-sider making another pitcher.

a good pub

I've been drinking for as long as I can remember. When I was a kid, my dad gave me sips of his lager. When I was lucky, I got a little glass of shandy—half beer, half lemonade. But my really formative drinking experiences all happened in pubs. Pubs are what I miss most about England: you finish work, you sit in a pub, and you drink with your friends. The ritual is ingrained in me. Without it, I feel like I'm missing a part of my body.

A proper English pub is not like a tavern or dive bar in the United States. It's not like anything else, anywhere. I feel a different energy when I pop in midday to a shabby bar in New York. Sure, English pubs can be dark and dingy and odd. But that's the fun bit. The familiar bit. You feel comfortable there, you kind of become a part of the furniture. Pubs are beautiful in their way—Victorian places lovingly battered by their customers.

At our regular pub in London, the carpet was pocked with fag holes. The once-pretty ceiling had yellowed from smoke. The toilet was a special kind of cold. My sister and I would spend all day there, smoking B&Hs, buying each other rounds of Carling's Black Label or wonderfully tepid cask ales, and having it out with the old men propped up at the bar with a paper. We didn't do much eating there, though occasionally we'd dig into a decent shepherd's pie. One pub that we went to a bit had a column in the middle that you could wrap your arms around, and if you climbed to the top, you'd get a free beer. Every now and then, after a few hours of people-watching and a couple of pints, we'd have a go. Never did make it, though.

CUCUMBER COOLER

I'm all for a soft drink, but I'd much rather have this emerald green beverage on a hot day. Refreshing and just a little sweet and bubbly, it's also delicious with a splash of vodka.   **makes 4 drinks**

1½ pounds English cucumbers
A very small handful of mint leaves
½ teaspoon Maldon or another flaky sea salt
2 tablespoons agave syrup
3 cups chilled seltzer
Ice cubes

Roughly chop the cucumbers, and puree them in a blender until smooth. Strain the puree through a fine-mesh sieve into a jug, gently and patiently smooshing and stirring the solids until you have about 2 cups cucumber juice; discard the solids. Cover with plastic wrap and keep it in the fridge until you need it.

Freeze a large pitcher and four Collins glasses till they go frosty.

Put the mint and salt in a large pitcher and muddle (mash) to release the mint's flavor. Pour in the cucumber juice, agave syrup, and seltzer and stir well.

Fill the glasses with ice and pour in the cucumber cooler.

FROZEN MOSCOW MULE

I once worked at a restaurant that made granita out of ginger beer, first freezing it, then chipping away until it was slushy. That got me thinking about one of my favorite drinks, the Moscow Mule, a combination of ginger beer, lime juice, and vodka. A frozen Moscow Mule is just the thing for a hot summer day, cold and spicy. (Be sure to use Fentimans ginger beer if you want it really spicy.) Come to think of it, you might want to make a double batch just in case.   **makes about 6 drinks**

4½ cups spicy ginger beer, preferably Fentimans

2 limes

About 9 ounces vodka

Pour the ginger beer into a medium baking dish. Use a Microplane grater to finely grate in the zest of 1 lime (be careful to avoid the white pith), and have a stir. Cover with plastic wrap and freeze overnight.

Just before you're ready to make the drinks, grab a sturdy fork (an old one is best, because you're going to be a bit rough with it) and start chipping away at the frozen ginger beer with the tines until it's all shaved looking, like a lovely slush.

Fill rocks glasses with the slush so it's almost overflowing (about ¾ cup), pour 1½ ounces of vodka into each one, and then, if need be, top off with a bit more of the slush so it towers above the rim.

Cut the remaining lime into wedges and squeeze one over each drink. Pop a stirrer or small straw into each glass and drink away.

GIN MARIE

Gin reminds me of my nan. There wasn't a holiday where she didn't show up with a bottle of Gordon's. Occasionally she even brought her own lemons to make sure she could have a gin and tonic just as she liked it. I like gin too. I'm especially fond of Old Tom gin, the slightly sweet kind that's come back into fashion of late. This cocktail is as refreshing as a gin and tonic but with some added complexity. When you shake it with crushed ice and pour it into your glass, you get a crunchy flotilla of crystals.

makes 1 drink

1 teaspoon maraschino liqueur, preferably Luxardo
⅛ teaspoon absinthe
2 dashes of Angostura bitters
2 ounces Ransom Spirits Old Tom Gin
Crushed ice
One 1½-inch strip lemon peel

Special Equipment
A cocktail shaker

Put your cocktail glass into the freezer till it goes frosty.

Combine the liqueur, absinthe, bitters, and gin in a cocktail shaker. Add crushed ice, pop on the top, and shake vigorously for about 15 seconds. Strain the cocktail into the chilled glass. Bend and pinch the lemon peel over the top to release a little of its oil. Drink up.

RYAN'S OLD-FASHIONED

A riff from The Pig's former head bartender, Ryan Gannon, this is how I like the time-less cocktail. No modern flair, just a bit of care. Taking a moment to swirl the crunchy sugar and bitters around the glass creates an aromatic orange film that ensures that you get a little hit of both the sugar and bitters in every sip. Add spicy rye and a big, slow-melting ice cube, and I'm quite happy. If you don't have the right ice cube tray, freeze water in small Dixie cups, Ryan's trick. **makes 1 drink**

1 teaspoon coarse raw sugar
4 dashes Angostura bitters
One 1½-inch strip lemon peel
One 1½-inch strip orange peel
2 ounces rye whiskey, preferably Old Overholt
A splash of seltzer
1 extra-large ice cube

Combine the sugar and bitters in a rocks glass and gently swirl the glass around so the sugar and bitters coat the inside all the way to the rim.

Bend and pinch the lemon and orange peel over the top to release a little of their oil, then rub the rim of the glass with them and drop them in. Add the rye and a splash of seltzer, give a little stir, and carefully add the ice cube. Drink up.

D3 - Saturday   x17

Cassoulet
My Curry + rice
Lamb meatballs
Chowder
Pea ; ham soup
tomato soup
Stuffed Veal
Skirt Steak
Sweetbreads
Succotash
Veal Breast
Chopped chix liver
Sausages x grind/stuff
roasted toms ; pepps
Stuffed mussels
Roasted chicken
Artichoke smash
+ oatmeal cookie

Chef:
curry + 2nd
Veal breast
tomato soup
Chowder
Sweet breads
roasted tom
Pea soup
chix liver
Cassoulet
s/v
Stuffed muss

Katharine'

roast chicken
Cook ham h
Cassoulet be
Marmalade /
meatballs
Succotash

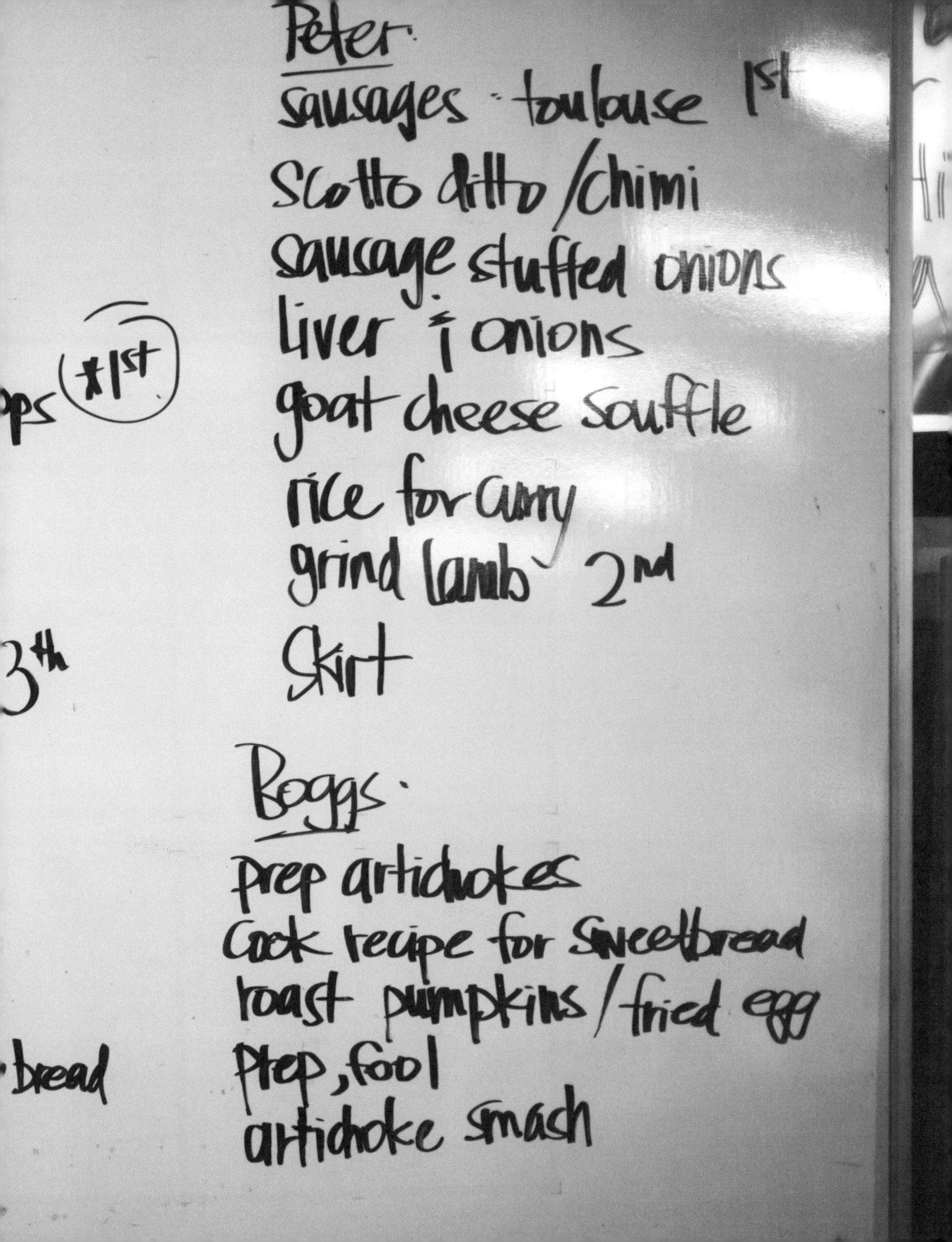

Peter:

sausages - toulouse 1st

scotto ditto /chimi

sausage stuffed onions

liver & onions

goat cheese souffle

rice for curry

grind lamb 2nd

Skirt

3th

ps (x1st)

Boggs:

prep artichokes

cook recipe for sweetbread

roast pumpkins / fried egg

prep, fool

artichoke smash

bread

sources

Most of the ingredients I call for in this book are best purchased from a farmers'
market or good butcher shop. A small bunch of pantry ingredients require a grocer
with an extensive cupboard. If you don't have one nearby, you can order many of
them online.

Anchovies (salt-packed)
Gustiamo.com

Maldon Salt
igourmet.com

Bottarga (mullet)
Gustiamo.com

Maple Syrup (bourbon-infused)
blisgourmet.com

Dried Beans
Ranchogordo.com

Marcona Almonds
Tienda.com

Dried Pequin Chilies
Melissaguerra.com

Old Tom Gin
Ransomspirits.com

Fennel Pollen and Fenugreek Seeds
Kalustyans.com

Polenta (Anson Mills and Cayuga Farms)
Ansonmills.com and shopcporganics.com

Kaffir Lime Leaves
importfood.com

Puy Lentils
Cybercucina.com

index

Note: Page numbers in italics refer to illustrations.

about the authors

APRIL BLOOMFIELD is the executive chef and co-owner with Ken Friedman of the Michelin-starred The Spotted Pig, The Breslin, and The John Dory restaurants. She has worked at The River Café in London and other celebrated restaurants. A native of Birmingham, England, she lives in New York City.

JJ GOODE writes about food for the *New York Times*, *Gourmet*, *Saveur*, *Bon Appétit*, *Food & Wine*, and *Every Day with Rachael Ray*. He is the coauthor of *Morimoto: The New Art of Japanese Cooking* with Masaharu Morimoto, which was nominated for a James Beard Award and won two IACP Awards; the *New York Times* bestseller *Serious Barbecue* with Adam Perry Lang; and *Truly Mexican* with Roberto Santibanez.

thank you